Praise for *Uncommon Greatness*

"Mark calls us to rise and then shows us how. Enlightening. Surprising. Essential."

—Dan Rockwell, Coauthor, *The Vagrant*;
AMA Top 50 Leader in Business; and Creator, *Leadership Freak* blog

"Too often as leaders, we get trapped in our own heads and stuck in pursuit of ordinary results. Part manifesto and part field guide, this book will help you set your sights higher and unlock greatness in others."

—Liz Wiseman, *New York Times* Bestselling Author,
Multipliers and *Impact Players*

"Mark Miller has discovered the secret for leaders. It's a different path, and it's not easy. But it's worth it. In *Uncommon Greatness*, Mark masterfully lays out the fundamentals of greatness and shows how we can design our preferred future and make a positive change in the world. It's the blueprint I wish I had when I started my professional journey."

—Jesse Cole, Owner, Savannah Bananas, and Author,
Fans First and *Find Your Yellow Tux*

"In *Uncommon Greatness*, Mark Miller primes the leader's mind to wonder what is possible. If you are looking for a resource to help you move from common to uncommon and really make a difference as a leader, I highly recommend you read this book."

—Heather R. Younger, Bestselling Author,
The Art of Active Listening and *The Art of Caring Leadership*

"Mark Miller knows that your ability to learn will determine your ability to lead. *Uncommon Greatness* is the result of Mark and his team investing decades of their lives to understand the commonalities among those who sustain greatness. Buy it, read it, and implement it. You and your team will be better for it."

—**Ryan Hawk**, Host of *The Learning Leader Show* podcast,
and Author, *Welcome to Management* and *The Pursuit of Excellence*

"If you want your leadership to make a difference in the world, if you care about excellence and performance results, you need to dive into this book to find out HOW. Prepare to be transformed!"

—**Cheryl Bachelder,** former CEO, Popeyes Louisiana Kitchen, Inc.,
and Author, *Dare to Serve*

"If you believe in fate, this book might not be for you. If you want to grow your leadership heart and skills to build the future and make a big difference in your organization and the world, Mark Miller has done that and shows how—wisely and delightfully."

–**Eduardo Briceño,** Author, *The Performance Paradox*

"The CEO who wants an uncommonly great company of people who go home happy after spending the day doing good work together would do well to make sure that this inspiring mindset is safely installed in their leadership. In his book *Uncommon Greatness*, Mark Miller's five essential leadership principles are within reach of everyone who sincerely aspires to make a positive difference in the lives of others."

—**Garry Ridge**, Chairman Emeritus, WD-40 Company,
and Executive Coach

"When most people think about greatness, they actually come up short of true greatness—the rare kind of greatness that leaves a lasting impact on the world. In *Uncommon Greatness*, Mark Miller shows us this kind of greatness is possible, achievable, and actually a lot closer than you think. But you've got to know the right fundamentals to get there. Thankfully, Mark teaches you those fundamentals along with exactly how you can pursue and instill them. Then you'll get to leave your own lasting impact on the world."

—**Matt Lyles,** Host, *The SIMPLE Brand* podcast

Uncommon
GREATNESS

ALSO BY MARK MILLER

Culture Rules
Smart Leadership

The High Performance Series

Chess Not Checkers
Leaders Made Here
Talent Magnet
Win the Heart
Win Every Day

Other Books

The Heart of Leadership
The Secret of Teams
*Great Leaders Grow**
*The Secret**

* Co-authored with Ken Blanchard

Un com mon
GREATNESS

Five
Fundamentals
to Transform
Your Leadership

MARK MILLER

Matt Holt Books
An Imprint of BenBella Books, Inc.
Dallas, TX

Matt Holt is an imprint of BenBella Books, Inc.
10440 N. Central Expressway
Suite 800
Dallas, TX 75231
benbellabooks.com
Send feedback to feedback@benbellabooks.com

BenBella and *Matt Holt* are federally registered trademarks.

Printed in the United States of America
10 9 8 7 6 5 4 3 2 1

Library of Congress Control Number: 2023040422
ISBN 9781637744703 (hardcover)
ISBN 9781637744710 (electronic)

Editing by Katie Dickman
Copyediting by Michael Fedison
Proofreading by Marissa Wold Uhrina and Jenny Bridges
Indexing by Amy Murphy
Text design and composition by Jordan Koluch
Author photo by Mary Caroline Russell
Printed by Versa Press

To Ken Blanchard—
Thanks for being a friend and mentor for the last twenty-five years!
When you asked me to co-author The Secret,
you changed the trajectory of my life and leadership.
Thanks for your continuing impact on the world!

Contents

FUNDAMENTAL #4:
VALUE RESULTS AND RELATIONSHIPS

FUNDAMENTAL #5:
EMBODY A LEADER'S HEART

A Note from the Author

I began writing almost a quarter century ago when Ken Blanchard and I teamed up to write *The Secret*, a book dedicated to the fundamental skills leaders need to be successful. We were excited to find a global audience for that work; today, over five hundred thousand copies of *The Secret* are in print in more than twenty-five translations around the world. The response to *The Secret* was encouraging, but we knew the message was incomplete.

As Ken and I acknowledged from the beginning, skills matter, but alone, they will never allow a leader to reach their full potential. That's why I decided to write a book dedicated to the topic of the leader's heart: *The Heart of Leadership*. To this day, I'm thankful to report, the content from this book continues to change lives by exposing and exploring the truth: *If your heart is not right, no one cares about your skills.*

The idea for *this* book was born in a question: If leadership skills and heart are both essential for a leader's success, why couldn't we create a single book to help leaders develop both?

Informed by what I've learned about leading people during a career spanning more than four decades, including some wins and a fair share of failures, combined with millions of dollars of research, *Uncommon Greatness* is my response to this question.

INTRODUCTION

Remember, all I'm offering is the truth—nothing more.

MORPHEUS

Do you believe in fate? Your answer matters more than you might imagine.

In *The Matrix* during their first meeting, Morpheus poses this question to Neo. Neo responds, "No, I don't like the idea that I'm not in control of my life."

Morpheus then offers Neo a choice: "Do you want the red pill or the blue one? Take the blue pill and you'll wake up in your bed and believe whatever you want to believe. Take the red pill and you stay in Wonderland, and I show you how deep the rabbit hole goes."

As Neo contemplates the options before him and their implications, Morpheus offers one final thought: "Remember, all I'm offering is the truth—nothing more."

Neo takes the red pill and Morpheus says, "Follow me."[1]

I want to ask you the same question Morpheus asked

Neo—not the red pill / blue pill question, but the other one: Do you believe in fate? If you do, this book is probably not for you.

Fate, by definition, means we have no agency in our lives, no influence, no opportunity beyond what has been preordained. However, if you want to know the truth about your personal potential and the path to achieve true greatness, I join Morpheus in saying, follow me and get ready for the ride of your life. Together, we will explore a realm you may have never considered, a new reality, and the path to get there.

Remember, all I'm offering you is the truth—nothing more.

THE PROMISE OF THIS BOOK

Uncommon Greatness is within your reach! How does that sound to you? Exciting? Like hyperbole? Outright crazy? I haven't even defined the term yet, but maybe, just maybe, I struck a chord— at least with the greatness part. Who wants to be mediocre? Not me, not you. Greatness sounds like a real stretch goal; you may be wondering if it's even possible.

Yes, as audacious as it may sound, greatness is available to every leader. But not just any form of greatness, Uncommon Greatness. You were born for greatness, even if you've never considered the possibility. You can literally change your world, and I'm going to show you how.

Together we will explore the five Fundamentals you'll need to study, practice, develop, and pursue the rest of your life as a leader. If leadership is your vocation, this quest for mastery will end when your career ends. For those who lead out of a sense of purpose, your journey will continue until your last breath. You retire from a job, not a calling.

The Fundamentals will enable you to tackle your most perplexing leadership challenges and lead individuals, teams, and your organization to new levels of accomplishment. They will also allow you to move to a new level of leadership and experience the joy, fulfillment, and results associated with Uncommon Greatness.

WHO IS THIS BOOK FOR?

Friends, colleagues, consultants, and mentors have been telling me for years that I need to narrow my target audience. The questions I've been asked include: Are you writing for senior leaders? Is your content intended for young leaders? First-time supervisors? Middle managers? I have always struggled to answer these questions. The reason I'm telling you all of this is simple: recently, I had a breakthrough.

This book, and all the resources I have created over the last twenty-five years, are for one subset of leaders, regardless of where they live, what language they speak, what level they currently occupy on their company's org chart, and with no regard to whether they've been leading for six months or sixty years. *Uncommon Greatness* was written to serve leaders who:

- Believe they can make a difference in their world.
- Care deeply about personal excellence.
- Are energized by producing tangible results.

Leaders are the architects of the future. As such, we have the opportunity to literally design and build a preferred future. And virtually every problem is a leadership problem—stemming from a leader's direct actions or lack thereof. So, given the unique role leaders have in creating the future, you are perfectly positioned to make the world, at least your world, a better place.

Leaders are the indispensable levers required for positive change in the world. Without good leaders, people and organizations flounder. No team or organization drifts to greatness; they must be led there.

OUR RESEARCH METHODOLOGY

As we explore each of the Fundamentals, we will draw on several sources of information, instruction, and inspiration.

Over the last two-plus decades, this content has been shared with hundreds of thousands of leaders around the world; their feedback is testimony to the efficacy and transformative power of this material.

More recently, we conducted rigorous quantitative research including a survey of more than four thousand leaders from six countries. These leaders represent numerous industries; come from small, medium, and large companies; are at all levels within their organizations; and have a wide range of experience.

All of this was bolstered by hundreds of hours of desk research and interviews with leaders who excel at their craft.

This process allowed us to do more than articulate each Fundamental in a succinct and hopefully compelling way. We have also identified scores of ideas that have worked for others as they applied the Fundamentals in real-world situations. That's why, after the introduction of each Fundamental, we have devoted an entire chapter to best practices and key strategies to help you apply what you just read about. I'm excited to share these with you and believe each idea is worth your full consideration.

The best practices and their accompanying strategies should *not* be viewed as a to-do list. These practices are descriptive, not prescriptive. If you decide to try some of the ideas, you'll want to adapt them for your situation. Also, be selective. There are far too many ideas for you to implement immediately—any attempt to do so would be disastrous. Finally, some of the ideas will not be applicable to your situation, at least not today. That's okay. The Ideas for Action chapters should be viewed as a resource you can return to as needed for years to come.

On the following pages you will also be exposed to scores of men and women who are exemplars of the strategies and tactics you'll need on your journey. However, I need to offer a quick disclaimer: I don't personally know the majority of the people you're going to read about. Therefore, I cannot say they are on the path to Uncommon Greatness. What I can say with complete confidence is they clearly demonstrate one or more of the ideas I am asking you to consider. Please don't let this caveat minimize the significance of the ideas they model for us all.

DO YOU WANT THE TRUTH?

The truth can be liberating or terrifying. As leaders, when we think about our potential to impact the world, maybe the truth is both. The truth is you are powerful. I want to help you leverage that strength for good in the world.

Here's another bit of truth: some of the ideas in this book are countercultural and have been for millennia. If you decide to continue reading, please do so with an open heart and an open mind. While many of you will be affirmed, others will be challenged at a deeply personal level. You will most likely be confronted with some new perspectives regarding your role and how you add value in the world. The ideas you are about to explore may flip your world upside down. You may even emerge with a new sense of calling.

I have invested more than four decades trying to lead every day better than I did the day before, with countless missteps along the way. I know firsthand that learning to lead can be a real challenge. However, I have a prediction to make—once you taste Uncommon Greatness, you will pursue it the rest of your life.

I hope you'll take the red pill and enjoy the journey!

CHOOSE A DIFFERENT PATH

*Two roads diverged in a wood, and I took the road
less traveled by, and that has made all the difference.*

ROBERT FROST

Quantuvis! Perhaps you encountered this word in Latin class? I didn't. Latin was reserved for the college-bound kids at my school, and I was on the vocational track. However, I have picked up a few Latin words and phrases over the years, none more profound in my life than *quantuvis*. It roughly translates to "as great as you determine (or choose)." If the word was not so obscure, it could have been the title of this book; if you want to be a great leader, you can be—but you must choose greatness.

If you do choose greatness, you'll immediately be confronted by your next choice: What's your definition of greatness? Before you think too long about your answer, let me help by telling you there are two forms: Common and Uncommon Greatness. Let's look at a few of their differences.

GREATNESS

Common	Uncommon
Focused on the achiever	Focused on others
Widely celebrated	Often unnoticed
Exalts individual excellence	Elicits excellence from others
Fleeting impact	Enduring value

Uncommon Greatness is evident by the impact the leader has on others, not the accolades bestowed on the leader along the way. This form of greatness releases untapped human potential allowing people and organizations to flourish. As a result of the leader's efforts, value is created and cascaded from one person to the next and the next, often for generations.

Uncommon Greatness is rare, but it has always been with us. You can find dazzling appearances throughout history and even today. You just must know what you're looking for to appreciate the impact these leaders had and have on the world. This elusive form of greatness is often hiding in plain sight. We will open your eyes on the pages that follow so that you can not only see it, but can also experience it in your world on a daily basis.

Many leaders are working to achieve common greatness only because they don't know of a higher level of achievement. And, make no mistake, the effects of personal achievement can be intoxicating. However, when you select the higher goal, you have the opportunity to transform the common to the uncommon.

For most leaders, your journey began with the pursuit of personal excellence—Uncommon Greatness makes no place for mediocrity. But personal excellence can be either a stumbling block or a stepping stone. The trap that ensnares so many is their inability to escape the grip of common greatness. If you allow yourself to be imprisoned by your own accomplishments, you will be excluded forever from the ranks of the leaders who have chosen to strive for the higher ground. Pursuing Uncommon Greatness requires a leap of faith—a shift in your head and your heart.

Far too many leaders have been misled and, consequently, they settle for the lesser good. Don't hear me say there is nothing appealing or noble about common greatness—it is still rare air. Most people never muster the energy and the diligence to achieve the lofty levels of accomplishment associated with common greatness. However, it is not the prize so many hope it will be. The stories of miserable, unfulfilled high achievers could fill volumes. Far too many leaders are climbing a ladder that is leaning against the wrong wall. One of the signs of their misguided efforts is loneliness. It's not lonely at the top if you take people with you.

For these leaders, their root problem is the goal to which they aspire—common greatness will always be a shallow victory. Only Uncommon Greatness can fill the void in our lives so many leaders are struggling to close. I intend to challenge, equip, and inspire you to never settle for mere common greatness again.

I trust the lists on page 8 were helpful in differentiating the two forms of greatness. The distinction between the two forms likely raises a question: As a leader, how do you shift your focus and ambition from Common to Uncommon Greatness? There is only one path.

UNCOMMON LEADERSHIP

An expanded view of leadership is required to approach Uncommon Greatness. Skills matter, they are foundational, but your heart matters even more. We must escape the gravitational pull of self-serving behaviors and focus our energy on releasing the untapped potential of those we serve. I've included both of these nonnegotiable elements in the Fundamentals that follow. Taken collectively, they will help you stay on course and maximize your contribution over a lifetime of leadership.

Several years ago, I had the opportunity to complete an assessment that came with a high-powered consultant to help me process my results. Although I had completed many assessments of this type over the years, I was pumped. I'm always excited for the opportunity to gain fresh perspective on how I might improve my leadership.

After the respondents' surveys were returned and tabulated, we scheduled a meeting to discuss the results. Honestly, when the consultant arrived in my office, he was undone. I could tell something was wrong, so I asked.

"Are you okay?"

"It's about your results . . ." he said.

"And . . . ?"

"When you walk into a room, you are not trying to take charge." He stopped.

"You are correct," I said. "What's your point?"

"Well, that's what leaders do . . . and you don't."

"When I walk in a room, I'm trying to figure out how I can add the most value. Sometimes that is to take charge and sometimes it is to take out the trash."

I'm convinced this guy is still confused today. He, like most of the world, is operating under a paradigm of mere common greatness where our greatest contributions are those situations in which we serve ourselves and showcase our talents. He is coaching leaders on how to achieve common greatness. By advocating for a limited and inferior form of leadership, he has missed the bigger opportunity and the truth.

As leaders, our highest value is realized when we do what is needed in the moment to serve others and the organizations that employ us. However, to achieve the humility and discipline to do what is needed rather than showcase our talents, we must learn to escape our own bias and the preconceived notions of others. To pursue Uncommon Greatness, leaders must constantly ask and answer this question: *How can I add the most value in this situation?*

Why this question, specifically? For me, it's a trigger for my mind and heart—a signal to override my natural tendencies. Far too often, my first instinct is to think about me first, not others. I don't think I'm alone. There is something in humans pushing and pulling us to prioritize our wants, needs, and desires above those of the people around us. This is not the way of Uncommon Greatness. By always seeking to add value for others, my focus shifts to those I have the opportunity to serve in that moment. This may be a good first step for you on your path toward Uncommon Greatness . . . How can you add value for people you encounter today?

Uncommon Greatness demands a choice to lead in an uncommon fashion, allowing our character and context to dictate our methods. It is an amalgamation of what the vision demands while never losing sight of the people who must make the vision a reality.

Uncommon Leadership is not a domain in which gender, race, age, educational level, or occupational boundaries should prevent you from excelling. Nor should our circumstances, our demographics, our level in an organization, or our station in life be seen as a reason to forgo Uncommon Greatness. We, as human beings, are the dominant impediment to our own greatness. Therefore, we control the vital levers of our future impact and influence.

THE GLOBAL LEADERSHIP CRISIS

As you look across the sweep of history, a vivid pattern emerges—leaders are at the heart of every major movement, revolution, institution, kingdom, nation, or organization ever formed. Leaders are the catalytic force for good. The lack of leadership can also be seen in the demise of civilizations, nations, institutions, and organizations. The future will be no different. Everything rises and falls on leadership. Armies, schools, hospitals, churches, families, businesses, and nations all are leader-dependent.

The problem: large numbers of leaders are not meeting the demands of the moment. As a result, they are jeopardizing the future of their organizations and our world. The signs of a global leadership crisis are everywhere.

- In a study covering 19 countries, Marcus Buckingham and his colleagues at ADP found only 15 percent of workers are fully engaged at work. This means 85 percent of the workforce is just showing up.[1]
- According to McKinsey, 80 percent of executives believe their business model is at risk to new innovations.[2]
- According to Gallup, 82 percent of managers aren't very good at leading people.[3]
- Forty percent of current frontline leaders do not feel equipped to lead well.
- Forty-five percent of leaders also lack the confidence to help their employees develop the skills they need.[4]
- Globally, the cost of poor management approaches $7 trillion—or 9 to 10 percent of the world's GDP.[5]
- Fifty percent of leaders do not believe they have enough emerging leaders to meet *future* demands of their organization.[6]
- Thirty-three percent of organizations do not have sufficient leaders for *today*.[7]

If you believe everything rises and falls on leadership, these facts reflect a perfect storm for the entire planet.

Our response to this crisis matters! A profound shift is needed—the traditional focus on common greatness will be insufficient to release the untapped potential resident in the people and organizations we serve. Common greatness is transactional; while, if we raise our sights, Uncommon Greatness is transformational. The pursuit alone will transform us, the people and organizations we serve, and our performance.

THE FUNDAMENTALS OF UNCOMMON LEADERSHIP

Now with the crisis clearly before us, let's turn our full attention to the focus of this book: helping you become an Uncommon Leader. Let's go back to my challenge for you to add value. Although there are infinite ways a leader can add value, some are far more strategic than others. The following Fundamentals of Uncommon Leadership represent five strategic ways every leader can and must add value, starting today.

Have you ever thought about what leaders actually do? Our team asked this question twenty-five years ago. We were overwhelmed by the number of things the best leaders do—hundreds, maybe a thousand or more specific activities. I remember the day well—we filled page after page of flip chart paper. We wallpapered the entire conference room from floor to ceiling with our findings. Obviously, leadership is a huge topic and encompasses a very large and complex set of competencies and skills. Our exercise validated the challenge, complexities, and enormity of the tasks leaders face on an ongoing basis.

Unfortunately, this realization created only a fleeting sense of accomplishment. On one hand, it helped us realize why our previous multiyear effort to articulate our leadership point of view had been so arduous. We had conducted interviews, explored global best practices, and, collectively, I'm guessing we also read over two hundred books on leadership. All of these efforts led to a moment of clarity: those we lead expect and deserve so much from us. Only when we faced the scope and scale of our responsibility could we begin to search for a more simplified way to tackle this gargantuan topic.

The question we asked was: Could we create a short list of the critical few things the best leaders consistently do? We did ultimately identify these competencies and called them the Fundamentals. They provide the structure for the balance of this book. Now, almost a quarter century later, I'm making only one tweak to our original list, which I'll explain in due time.

The following is a summary of the Fundamentals of Uncommon Leadership. We'll do a deep dive into the spirit, intent, and ideas for action for each of these in the pages that follow.

See the Future—*To weave the threads of what you know to be true and what you want to be true into a compelling picture of a better tomorrow.*

Leadership always begins with a picture of the future. What are you trying to accomplish? Where are you trying to take the people on your team or in your organization at large? Why is the journey necessary? The future you envision will be informed by your experience, intuition, creativity, judgment, and more. Leaders must be able to describe their preferred future with sufficient detail to rally people to pursue it.

Engage and Develop Others—*To help those you lead care deeply about their work, coworkers, and the organization while fueling their growth along the way.*

Engagement is the precursor to elite levels of sustained performance. Without it, the most you can expect are flashes of
brilliance. Engagement has two different forms. First, who do
you invite, or engage, to join you on the journey? Next, what do
you do to ensure these people really care? How much they care
about their work, their coworkers, and the organization is largely
up to you.

Reinvent Continuously—*To routinely escape the bounds of the
present and the known in pursuit of improved skills, methods, and
outcomes.*

All progress is preceded by change. Change is at the heart
of our role as leaders. Not change for change's sake—change
in service of growth, performance, and the vitality of our organization and those we lead. Change is not a distraction or an
inconvenience—change is the primary lever at our disposal to
determine our success, failure, or irrelevance. We are responsible
for and expected to help create and sustain positive change. Your
present reality has been greatly influenced by your current and
past practices. Therefore, if you want different outcomes, you'll
need to change something. Reinvention is a core and reoccurring
theme among the most successful leaders.

Value Results and Relationships—*To successfully navigate the
challenges of honoring those we lead while ensuring sustained levels
of elite performance.*

There is a way to maximize results and it's not what most
leaders think. To focus exclusively on results will, over time,

suboptimize them. The ability to focus on results *and* relationships is the key many leaders have been looking for. When leaders embrace both, tremendous power is released within an organization. This is the classic example of what the former Stanford professor, author, and leadership expert Jim Collins calls the "genius of the and." There is tension inherent when you embrace both, and this tension should never be resolved—it must be managed.[8]

Embody a Leader's Heart—*To live and lead in a fashion that makes you a leader people want to follow.*

Think about a leader whom you admire. What is it about them that brings them to mind? If you make a list of their attributes, I'm guessing you'll include something about their heart—traits, characteristics, or attributes that transcend their skill set. Yes, skills matter, but as we'll explore in more detail, skills alone are never sufficient. If your heart is not right, no one cares about your skills. We'll explore some traits and characteristics that will set you apart and be the real differentiator for Uncommon Leaders. Your heart can be developed, and it must be. Your efficacy as a leader hangs in the balance. If you fully embrace this fundamental, you can become a leader people want to follow.

THE WORLD NEEDS YOU

The Fundamentals of Uncommon Leadership are the keys to unlock Uncommon Greatness in you and those around you. But to what end? Why should anyone want to accept the role and responsibility to lead others? Because you can change the world.

I have long talked about the power of leaders to change the

world. However, for the pages that follow, I want to narrow my challenge. Don't think about changing *the* world. Think about how the ideas represented here can help you change *your* world. When you change yours and I change mine, and leaders everywhere do the same, collectively, we can change *the* world.

Fundamental #1

SEE THE FUTURE

SEE THE UNSEEN

The best way to predict the future is to create it.

PETER DRUCKER

While studying at Princeton University in 1989, Wendy Kopp saw something others did not see— the potential impact of a passionate group of very sharp, recent college graduates, focused on the problem of educational inequity. As her thoughts took shape and her passion grew, Kopp captured her vision in her senior thesis.[1]

Kopp envisioned a 1960s-era Peace Corps–type organization focused on serving underresourced children in the inner cities. She believed these recruits could make the greatest impact by serving as teachers. In her paper she outlined her dream for the organization that would become Teach For America (TFA): "One day, all children in this nation will be able to attain a great education."[2]

Although her faculty advisor liked the idea, he was skeptical Kopp could secure funding for such an endeavor. He wrote off her proposal as an "intellectual exercise." What the advisor failed to grasp was the power and clarity of the vision and Wendy's passion to make it a reality. A bold vision will always be challenged and dismissed by some. Many cannot imagine what the leader has envisioned. Leaders see the unseen, and then work to make it a reality for all to see.[3]

As graduation approached, Kopp knew she needed a job and began interviewing for roles on Wall Street and in a large consulting firm. However, her heart was not in either of these places; she was more convinced than ever that her idea could make a difference. She had seen a preferred future, and nothing was going to stop her from trying to make it a reality.

In the spring of her senior year, she met with executives from some of the nation's largest corporations to discuss her plan. Her vison fueled her tenacity and single-mindedness. Her efforts slowly began to pay off. Union Carbide offered her free office space in New York City, and Mobil Oil gave her a seed grant to cover her living expenses as she continued to seek funding and partnerships. With each step, Kopp's vision moved closer to becoming a reality.[4]

After graduation in 1989, Kopp moved to NYC and over the summer recruited a board of directors, continued to raise funding, and hired four staff members. Morgan Stanley, Ross Perot, and others stepped up, and Teach For America was born.[5]

Educational inequity was not a new problem; Wendy knew this. And the data has continued to be clear and compelling for many years. There is an undisputable link between poverty and the quality of the education students receive. We won't revisit the data from the last century; let's just take a quick look at more modern times:[6]

- Students from low-income families dropped out of high school at twice the rate of higher-income families in 2017.
- Eighteen percent of black eighth graders are proficient or above in reading or math, compared with 47 percent of white eighth graders.
- Twenty-three percent of Latino eighth graders are proficient or above in reading or math, compared with 47 percent of white eighth graders.
- There is a two-year gap in reading and a one-and-a-half-year gap in math between fourth graders growing up in poverty and their higher-income peers.
- There is a three-year gap in reading—and more than a three-year gap in math—between eighth graders growing up in poverty and their higher-income peers.

Numbers like these were catalytic for Wendy. Her plan involved creating an elite force for good. Candidates for the teacher roles would be subjected to a rigorous selection process and, if selected, make a two-year commitment to the program. They would be trained and assigned to a city. Once on the ground, these students had to apply to be teachers, be interviewed, and be selected by local school leaders.

Over the years since the organization's inception, the large number of applicants and the low selection rate point to both the desire many young people have to make a difference in the world and Teach For America's high standards. In 2003, of the 15,708 applicants, TFA selected only 1,600, yielding an acceptance rate of 10 percent.[7] The selection percentage has remained relatively consistent over the years while the number of interested young

people has climbed. In 2017, 49,000 applications were received
and only 3,500 were selected. This translates to an acceptance
rate of about 7 percent.[8]

In addition to serving the students in underserved and underresourced areas, Kopp has been unapologetic about the long
game she is pursuing. She has always maintained that one of
her objectives is to prepare the next generation of leaders in education, going as far as saying in a Seattle radio interview in
2001 that TFA was a "leadership development organization, not
a teaching organization." She believes that long-term systemic
change will ultimately be required to usher in the substantive
and sustainable changes education in America needs. She is
counting on her alumni to lead this charge.[9]

Comments like the one above raised the ire of some teachers
who are not part of TFA. Some use Kopp's words to suggest her
organization is not concerned with the education of the children in the classroom. The data would suggest otherwise. Even
though the outcome metrics between TFA teachers and others is
often limited, as a group, students taught by Kopp's teachers do
outperform others in many situations. However, back to Kopp's
long game concerning educational reform, the real impact of
TFA may not be realized for years to come.

According to data released a few years ago, 65 percent of
Teach For America's alumni were working in education and 84
percent of them were working in low-income areas. These are the
seeds of change Kopp envisioned from the outset.[10]

I'll offer a quick editorial comment about the naysayers.
Any significant, transformational vision will encounter opposition. Be prepared! If you are attempting to do something big
and bold, and certainly if you are attempting something untried,

do not be surprised when you encounter opposition. I would be concerned if you don't.

Today, Kopp has transferred the CEO role for TFA and has moved on to extend her vision to the world. In 2007, she founded Teach For All and is now serving schools and children in more than fifty countries.[11] Kopp's story of growing global impact is a glowing testimony to the power of a leader who can see the unseen!

SEE THE FUTURE

One of the things that leaders are required to do is See the Future. Kopp is an outstanding example of what can happen when leaders step up and see the unseen. This is not only what people need from us as leaders but also what they expect. This expectation comes in many forms.

- We are expected to see the changing landscape in our industry—before it changes.
- We are asked to see the outcome of potential strategies years before the final verdict can be rendered.
- We're expected to see the potential in people before that potential has been translated into performance.
- We must have a picture of the future we are attempting to create for our organization—we must have vision.

For some leaders and aspiring leaders, this Fundamental is daunting. Whether Seeing the Future energizes you or terrifies you, it will be this Fundamental that allows you to enter the ranks of true leadership. Real leadership always begins with a picture of the future. If you've read anything about leadership, you'll know this picture of the future is often referred to as vision. Vision is an indispensable ingredient for effective leadership.

Leaders have the opportunity and the responsibility to answer questions such as:

- What are we trying to accomplish?
- What are we trying to become?
- What does the preferred future look like?
- How will we measure our progress?
- Why should we pursue this vision?
- What are the consequences if we do not pursue the vision?

As you think deeply about the answers to questions like these, the future you desire will often emerge. It is the synthesis of your responses where your preferred future can often be found. Your future is out there awaiting your focused energy and passion to make it a reality.

Why would a leader withhold the destination from those who must rally to make the vision a reality? Although I attempted to answer this question in my book *Culture Rules*, I know some of you haven't read it yet. Therefore, I've chosen to repeat a few of those thoughts here.

The leader doesn't have a vision. Seeing the unseen is extremely difficult and requires a blend of foresight, courage, creativity, optimism, and time. For many leaders, they have not invested the time to formulate their own vision of the future. This lack of clarity can be paralyzing for a leader and an organization. You cannot share what you do not know.

The leader doesn't know how to make the vision a reality. In this case, the leader may have a fairly good idea of the future they would like to create. The root problem is they do not know how the organization will get there. This is very common. Even the best leaders rarely know the exact "how" when they declare the "where." Mapping the specific details of the journey ahead will in most situations require the collective wisdom of the organization. The leader should not feel the pressure to have all the answers. Often, the leader's greatest contribution after the destination is clear will be the questions they ask, not the answers they provide.

The leader fears failure. Fear makes cowards of us all. Leaders often fail—sometimes in small things, sometimes in big things. But leaders try. Leadership is rarely about certainty. All we can be certain about are our intentions and the level of effort we will expend. We must face our fear and lead.

Leaders must overcome these challenges and share a compelling picture of the future with those they wish to lead. In the section that follows we'll see several examples we can learn from as we See the Future.

BOOKS AND BEYOND

Jeff Bezos is a brilliant guy with formal training in electrical engineering and computer science, but he is much more than that. He's also a visionary leader and an entrepreneur. He has pushed the limits of what is possible and has changed the way our world works.

Bezos didn't invent the internet, but he certainly saw its potential. In 1994, Bezos was a hedge fund manager working in New York. He imagined the world's largest selection of books readily available to a waiting world.[12] He saw what others could not—the future of the internet as a hub for commerce.

The vision was strong, and sales were growing, but profitability proved elusive. After seven long years in business, in the first quarter of 2001, Amazon posted its first profits. The growing revenue and, ultimately, profitability allowed Bezos to expand his vision. Today, the company is a leader in cloud services and streaming. They're also a major player in content production. They have won numerous Academy Awards, Emmys, Golden Globe Awards, and Screen Actors Guild recognition.[13]

In 2000, Bezos launched another chapter in his growing legacy. Once again, he saw what many others had only speculated about—the opportunity for private industry to harness the vastness of space. Inspired by the possibilities, he founded Blue Origin, a private company conceived to make space accessible to a larger number of people. The name was conceived with a nod to the blue sky we enjoy on a clear day and a desire to protect our planet.

Early research and development efforts focused on reusable rocket technology. Blue Origin's first big public success came in 2015 when they successfully launched and landed a suborbital rocket. In 2021, the company sent its first crewed mission into space. Bezos was on the crew. The ship reached an altitude of more than one hundred kilometers, or sixty-two miles. NASA has now turned to Blue Origin to help develop technology and hardware to return humans to the moon. Currently, Blue Origin is working on several projects, including plans for a lunar lander.[14]

What's next for Bezos? With total market capitalization exceeding $1 trillion in 2023, the sky's the limit for a leader like Bezos who can see the unseen and make it a reality. Who knows? Maybe the sky is not the limit.

There is a pattern in Bezos's story. It's something all of us can learn from—leadership always begins with a picture of the future. And the picture will be challenged by many, even considered absurd by others. Let's face it, when the leader begins to talk about the future, they are trading on our imagination and, in many cases, our fears. The future does not yet exist; this is why so many view leaders as not being grounded in reality. We are trying to *create* a *future* reality. To See the Future requires courage, creativity, intuition, judgment, discernment, and more. I know for many of you this list of attributes feels overwhelming. Don't shrink back! The world needs you, your vision, and your leadership.

YOUR VISION

In a chapter showcasing visionaries like Wendy Kopp and Jeff Bezos, I don't want you to be discouraged or feel limited by your circumstances. Their stories are intended to inspire, not diminish, your dreams. I am confident in your ability to make great things happen in this world.

Beyond inspiration, stories like the ones we just read also cause me to reflect: Is my vision big enough? I believe this is a question leaders should ask often.

I'm reminded of a time almost a decade ago when I had my vision expanded. We had just made the decision to radically change our strategy for leadership development in our organization. Rather than focusing on serving a relatively small group of leaders, I was challenged by our CEO to find a way to serve ten million leaders a year.

This new challenge stretched my thinking and required an

entirely new strategy. Today, I've long since ditched the idea of serving only ten million leaders; my new goal is to serve one hundred million leaders over the next few years. As you would expect, some have told me I'm crazy while I'm sure many others are thinking I am even if they won't say it to me directly. Interestingly, others have challenged me that one hundred million may be far too low a goal in today's world with the power and reach of social media continuing to grow. Therefore, I've amended my vision, now calling one hundred million leaders served a milestone. In the coming months and years, I will not be surprised if a larger, more audacious goal emerges.

Whatever your vision, think big and then bigger!

READY TO LEAD?

As you read my challenge to think big and then bigger, some of you are feeling a little unsure. You may have questions about your ability to see a bigger future; others are wondering if you can pull it off. This is understandable. Are you ready? Readiness is often forged in the crucible of leading.

Benki Pyánko was only ten years old when his father, the tribal chief, passed away. In keeping with the traditions of the Ashaninka people, he would immediately assume responsibility for their tribe. His people lived in the Amazon region of South America with sprawling lands in Peru and Brazil. Benki's village was so remote it took days to reach by canoe.[15]

The primary challenge the young leader faced was illegal logging. Their forest was being devastated right before their eyes. Benki had an intuitive sense that preserving and restoring the forest was his highest priority. When he was eighteen, he left his village for the first time, traveling three thousand miles to Rio de Janeiro to attend the Earth Summit—a gathering sponsored by the United Nations Conference on Environment and Development. At the 1992 event, Benki talked with leaders about the devastation to the Amazon rainforest and their homeland. In return for his stories, leaders shared with him new ideas and technologies, and connected him to resources.[16]

Returning to his village, Benki had connected his people to the outside world. Armed with new information, Benki began to lead change with his people. In 1993, Benki created the Apiwtxa Association, named after his village. This group enabled him to defend his culture while working to protect and restore their ecosystem. His focus was on reforestation and building agroforestry systems to ensure both food and economic autonomy for his people.[17]

Since Benki's first trip to the outside world, his village has been able to build schools, diversify their sources of livelihood, and begin reforestation—restoring 25 percent of the land destroyed by the loggers. Under his leadership, the people have even embraced satellite technology that is allowing them to monitor the health and security of their treasured rainforest. Over the years, Benki also learned to speak both English and Portuguese to better champion their cause.

When asked about his role in this unbelievable story, Benki says he is trying to preserve the forest for his grandchildren the way his grandfather did for him. Core to his success was a compelling vision. What's yours? Leadership always begins with a picture of the future. Only then do you have the opportunity to rally others to make the vision a reality.

Even in the face of uncertainty and opposition, if you want

to really lead, you must know where you are going. To See the Future is the most fundamental of the Fundamentals. It is essential to establish your North Star just as these leaders in this chapter demonstrated. Ask yourself, where are you attempting to take your would-be followers? If you need help figuring that out, the next chapter is for you.

Do you feel ready to lead? I can only begin to imagine how the young Benki must have felt. Clearly, he was not ready to lead, but he led regardless. Over the course of your lifetime, you should constantly find yourself wrestling with similar feelings, asking, "Am I ready?"

The best leaders are comfortable being uncomfortable. We should always be working on problems bigger than our calendar and our checkbook can support. This is where we'll find personal growth and new frontiers for our organization. The reward you receive for solving a problem is a bigger problem to solve. The Fundamentals we are exploring throughout this book will help. They are timeless and universally applicable, even in the jungles of the Amazon.

Try This: How are you doing on this first Fundamental? Have you developed the ability to See the Future? Our team has created a FREE assessment to help you discover your next steps as you work to improve your leadership. All you have to do is text **uncommon** to 66866 or scan the QR code in the Resources section at the end of the book. If you want help assessing your current reality across all the Fundamentals, I believe this tool will help.

SEE THE FUTURE: IDEAS FOR ACTION

For many leaders, the opportunity to See the Future is the most fulfilling part of their role; for others, it is their nemesis. Regardless of whether you find this Fundamental energizing or draining, you must figure out how to see the unseen—we, as leaders, are the architects of tomorrow. If we can't see it, our organizations can't build it.

In order to See the Future, it will be helpful if you **Remember the Past**, **Remain Grounded**, and **Dare to Dream**. Let's take a deeper look at each of these best practices and related strategies.

REMEMBER THE PAST

What lessons from your past can you harness for your advantage in the future? I promise you they are there. Socrates said, "The unexamined life is not worth living."[1] The best leaders always learn from the past but they never live there. The following strategies can help.

Listen to the Founders. The founder(s) of your organization saw something—an opportunity, an unmet need, a confluence of forces, something. They had an idea, an insight, or an impulse to do something, and they did! From that catalytic moment, your organization was born. As you think about the future, what can you learn from your founder(s)? Do you need more courage? Do you need to listen to your customers more intently to discern their needs? Certainly, our founders were human with both strengths and weaknesses. How did they leverage their strengths? How did they mitigate their weaknesses? Were their strategies successful? Have you read what they wrote during their tenure? Their speeches? The letters they wrote to the stakeholders? Read the interviews they did with the media too. If they wrote a book, you should read it—again. Periodically, you should immerse yourself in their work. You will probably be surprised by what you find.

Create a Milestones Map. A firm grasp of the past prepares you to create a better tomorrow. There have been wins, losses, seasons of stability, challenges, new products, mergers, leadership transitions, and much more. Do you have a firm grasp of the totality of your organization's history? You need to. The best leaders are steeped in the past in order to leverage it for their advantage in the future. Is there a rhythm evident in the past? What is the pace of innovation? How has the organization responded historically to adversity? What patterns exist? Have mergers and new products created the positive impact you desired?

Recounting the past is valuable at many levels. History always holds a deeper, richer reality than the facts alone are capable of revealing. The psychologists call this *historicity*. This level of awareness transcends the events of history and considers the underlying forces at play, the bias, prejudice, and interdependencies that created the past. Every leader should strive to understand not only what happened, but why.

Create a written timeline, preferably on a very large space—a whiteboard or roll of butcher paper will do nicely. Identify the milestones since the founding of your organization. If you think it was important, list it. Include the items I mentioned above and also include sales milestones, new plants coming online, the sale of a division, the date your plants became unionized, an explosion in a factory, a major reorganization, a major lawsuit against your company, a new competitor, an industry award, your tenth anniversary, a patent for a new product, a new IT system, a major shift in strategy, and anything else that comes to mind as potentially noteworthy.

Finally, step back and take a look. What do you see? What can you learn? Has the key to recovery from challenge always been innovation or leadership transition? How long is it typically between major accomplishments? What are the historical catalysts for these peaks? What might you do to bend the success curve going forward? What clues exist in your past that might accelerate your success in the future?

Do After-Action Reviews. Although a look at your historical challenges is helpful, there is no substitute for learning in real time. What are you doing today to make tomorrow better? One of the most powerful mechanisms leaders have at their disposal is the After-Action Review (AAR). This concept was popularized by the military but has huge upside potential for any organization with the discipline to embrace it.

I've explored this topic with senior military leaders, and they are in complete agreement on the power of the pause—deliberately and intentionally taking time to assess, in almost real time, what just happened and extracting lessons from it. The magic of the AAR is not to place blame for failure or shortcomings but to inform future actions.

There are typically four parts to an AAR:[2]

- What was expected to occur?
- What really happened?
- What went wrong and why?
- What went well and why?

The real world provides an unparalleled classroom for the observant student. There is little excuse for blindly repeating failures of the past. Cicero said, "Any man can make a mistake; only a fool keeps making the same mistake."[3] The AAR is a proven tool to create better outcomes.

After your next sales call, presentation, event, or project launch, conduct an AAR. Look for ideas to help you learn from the past to create a better future.

REMAIN GROUNDED

In *Smart Leadership*, I made the case to Confront Reality as the first Smart Choice that enables a leader to scale their impact. I stand by that. Only when we are grounded in truth can we lead from a position of strength. Unfortunately, this is much easier to say than to do. The more responsibility you have in an organization and the higher you have climbed the structural ladder, the more difficult it will be for you to know the truth.

In our recent surveys of leaders around the world, we

discovered a perception gap of about forty points between senior leaders and frontline associates on multiple topics. The gap exists when evaluating the success of change efforts, recommending your organization as a great place to work, or even the level of excitement about going to work. I'm sure if we explored more topics, this gap would persist. Leaders, particularly senior leaders, are typically out of touch with the reality of many of the people in their organization. If you are not grounded in reality, your warped perception of your current state is a huge liability as you think about your preferred future and the path to get there. Here are some ideas to consider as you seek to be grounded in reality.

Maintain a Customer Bias. Customers are the lifeblood of any organization. It's very difficult to over-listen to the voice of your customers. What formal mechanisms does your organization have in place to listen to your customers? How frequently do you listen? What happens to the information? How much weight and value do you give to the voice of the customer? Do you employ both quantitative and qualitative methods? When was the last time you personally attended a focus group with your customers?

If you don't have formal mechanisms in place to listen to your customers, commission someone to begin a pilot. See what you learn. If you don't have any focus groups scheduled, put one on the calendar. You can either host it yourself, or, if you have the resources, hire a professional. I recommend hiring a professional. If you do host it yourself, ask open-ended questions, do not be defensive—constructive feedback is a gift—and take really good notes. Remember, without customers, you have no organization. Cherish them and their input.

Beyond listening, what else can you do to maintain a

customer-biased view of the world? At Amazon, many of their teams add an empty chair in their meetings to represent the customer. This subtle prompt is intended to raise the question, "What would the customer say about this?"

Never lose sight of your customer. They pay the bills and give you the opportunity to exist as an organization.

Go and See for Yourself. Reality is easily distorted. The fact that leaders are generally not grounded in reality is typically not part of a nefarious plot to keep the leader in the dark or placate their fantasies about the world around them. Often, this is a matter of circumstance. In many cases, time and distance are the leading culprits creating the illusion of reality but in truth bearing little resemblance to the facts. As a practical matter, it is impossible for delusional, out-of-touch leaders to lead well. That's why this idea of Remaining Grounded in Reality is so critical.

Of all the strategies you can conceive for staying grounded, none will ever replace the practice of going to see for yourself. This is why the best leaders dedicate a portion of their busy schedules to hitting the road, many traveling around the world to see firsthand what is really happening closest to the work, the workers, and the customers.

When was the last time you "went to the field"? When will you go again? Is it on your calendar? I hesitate to recommend a frequency because every situation is unique. However, I have met very few leaders in my career who I would say spent too much time on the front lines. Generally speaking, more time is better.

One more tip for your consideration: stay longer than you feel appropriate. I've noticed a strange phenomenon as I have visited our locations over the years. Whether announced or un-announced, whether anonymous or in my official role, the longer

I stay, the more I learn. The longer you are present, the more likely you are to see things, hear things, and have people open up to you on issues they might never broach on a quick stop-in visit.

Listen Broadly and Proactively. Who do you listen to? Do you have a network of trusted advisors? I trust you listen to your inner circle—your leadership team. Who else? Do you have a coach? Mentors? A personal board of directors? I have no doubt you listen to your customers. I'm also confident you listen to your employees. Here's the point of this line of thinking: you need to listen to more than your gut. Your instincts matter, and at the end of the day, you, as the leader, will make a lot of decisions. However, is your intuition informed? If so, by whom? Here's another question: Is your listening strategic or sporadic? Are you proactive or reactive? I know some organizations do exit interviews with employees—fine. How many employees are you interviewing *before* they decide to leave? You need to listen broadly and proactively.

Make a list of all the audiences (voices) you would like to listen to over the course of a typical year. Indicate the frequency with which you engage each group. What could you do to be more proactive and strategic? Pay special attention to any gaps in audience or frequency as you map out your Strategic Listening Plan for the next twelve months.

DARE TO DREAM

What is your dream? This is not the same as a spreadsheet on which you compute a modest compounded growth rate over the next decade. Is there something bold in your future? If not, could there be? What about the future excites you? What challenges you? What will enliven your organization? The answers to these questions, and others like them, could illuminate your dream.

Elongate Your Perspective. Unless leaders are diligent, we will allow time compression to compromise our future. The best decisions are almost always made with a long view in mind. Many leaders appear to understand this better on a personal level than for their organizations. Look no further than 401(k) contributions. People with a long view and an understanding of compounding are quick to sign up for the program. Not because of how much cash they will have on hand in five years, but because they realize how much they will accumulate over the next thirty years. Vision is like this. When visions are big and bold, your initial progress may feel small, and it may be minor in the short term. But to pursue something so big it will take a lifetime to achieve can change your thinking, your energy, and your actions today.

This is one of the challenges with the way Wall Street works. Leaders forced to hit quarterly numbers often make short-term decisions with dire long-term consequences. One of my friends and mentors is John Maxwell, the internationally recognized leadership expert. John challenged me with the idea that too many leaders overestimate what they can accomplish in a day and underestimate what they can accomplish in a decade.

When Seeing the Future, imagine you are looking at the health indicators for your organization a decade from now, maybe two decades—elongate your perspective. What metrics would you look for to determine the overall health of the organization? With these metrics in mind, what strategies and tactics do you need to embrace today?

Identify the Risks of Not Changing. There is something

scarier than change—attempting to stay the same. We live in a dynamic world. No organization has the luxury of maintaining the status quo. The risks of irrelevance are real and ever present. Brands once thought of as immortal have ceased to exist. You've probably heard this stat before, but let me remind you of a staggering reality—success is not guaranteed:

> Comparing the 1955 *Fortune 500* companies to the 2019 *Fortune 500*, there are only 52 companies that appear in both lists and have remained on the list since it started. In other words, only 10.4% of the *Fortune 500* companies in 1955 have remained on the list during the 64 years since in 2019, and more than 89% of the companies from 1955 have either gone bankrupt, merged with (or were acquired by) another firm, or they still exist but have fallen from the top *Fortune 500* companies (ranked by total revenues) in one year or more.[4]

You cannot afford to stay the same; if you do, you are most likely on a long, slow death march as an organization. The good news: your organization has you, and you know your nonnegotiable responsibility as a leader is to create a better tomorrow.

Make a list of all the potential and probable negative outcomes if your organization does not pursue a bold vision. If this is a difficult exercise for you and your team, take a page from Dr. Edward de Bono and his six thinking hats.[5] Ask everyone on your team to, intentionally and deliberately, put on their "Black Hat" and imagine the worst possible outcome if you attempt to maintain the status quo. For some on your team, this will require a significant shift in thinking. For others, I'm guessing this will not be a challenge. After you've made a lengthy list, you can have a conversation regarding which of these risks you can mitigate by pursuing a bold vision.

Imagine the Possibilities. The future is probably my favorite facet of leadership. Just imagine what is possible! We are living in the most exciting time in the history of the world with unprecedented access to information and technology. Leaders have never had the resources at their disposal that we have today. What will limit your future? I believe the greatest threat to a better world is a lack of imagination on the part of leaders.

I recently met Jesse Cole, owner of the Savannah Bananas baseball team. Clearly, they are not your typical baseball team. They have created their own brand of the sport with a focus on increasing both fan engagement and the entertainment value of the event. The result: every game is sold out, they have a waiting list of five hundred thousand people who want to attend a game, and they have more than a million followers on Instagram. Among their unconventional strategies are the elimination of outside advertisers and the food and drinks are included in the ticket price—$25 per person as of this writing.

Jesse shared his personal discipline of generating ten new ideas every day. This has been his practice for more than a decade. Jesse is the first to admit that the majority of his ideas are not good—he cites the human pinata and grandma beauty pageants as prime examples.[6] However, many of his ideas have been good, with an occasional great one thrown in. Two that can be credited as big winners: games are limited to two hours and if a fan catches a foul ball, the batter is out. The best way to find an amazing, game-changing idea is to create a lot of ideas. Just imagine what you and your organization could accomplish over the next five, ten, even twenty years. Imagine the possibilities!

If you don't have one already, start a "What if . . . ?" list. Every day, add at least one idea to your list, or you can aim high like Jesse and set a goal to add ten ideas to your list every day.

———————

To See the Future is a privilege, an opportunity, and a huge responsibility. For some, this may feel a bit overwhelming. Work though the Ideas for Action you just reviewed and hold the future loosely.

One of the truths about the future that is rarely discussed is the fluid nature of the leader's vision. Don't fixate on the minute details of the future. A broad brush will do; the team will help fill in the details. Take comfort in the fact that the vision will most likely change over time—the strategy and tactics certainly will. A good-faith effort and the fortitude to do the work in the face of opposition will be critical.

Leadership always begins with a picture of the future. The people you need to enroll to create the future have a deep-seated and core question: *Where are we going?* Only the leader can answer this question—you are the leader.

SEE THE FUTURE
BEST PRACTICES AND KEY STRATEGIES

Remember the Past
- Listen to the Founders
- Create a Milestones Map
- Do After-Action Reviews

Remain Grounded
- Maintain a Customer Bias
- Go and See for Yourself
- Listen Broadly and Proactively

Dare to Dream
- Elongate Your Perspective
- Identify the Risks of Not Changing
- Imagine the Possibilities

Fundamental #2

ENGAGE AND DEVELOP OTHERS

BECOME UNSTOPPABLE

*Somewhere along the way, we must learn that
there is nothing greater than to do something for others.*

MARTIN LUTHER KING JR.

B ill Campbell began his career as a football coach, but on this day, his eulogy would be offered on a field in California thousands of miles from where he played in his early days. In attendance was a rare gathering of industry titans and regular working-class people. Those gathered included Larry Page, Sergey Brin, Mark Zuckerberg, Sheryl Sandberg, Tim Cook, Brad Smith, and Ben Horowitz. Also present was a waiter from a restaurant Bill frequented in New York, his favorite caddie from a golf course in Mexico, and many others. In all, an estimated two thousand people attended his funeral in 2016. The attendees had at least one thing common—they all loved Bill.[1]

Bill played football at Columbia University. After his playing days were over, he found himself back at his alma mater as the team's head coach. Bill had an inauspicious career there (12-41-1 over five seasons). At this point in his career journey, he turned his attention to business. This decision would define his legacy as an elite coach on a different playing field.

Bill made several unlikely career leaps after leaving the gridiron. He first moved to advertising, working for the legendary advertising agency J. Walter Thompson. Next stop, Kodak. While in this role, he met John Sculley, then the CEO of PepsiCo. Scully would later recruit Campbell to join him at Apple in the early '80s.

Once on the West Coast, Bill was instrumental in challenging the Apple board with the release of the iconic 1984 Super Bowl commercial in which a lone champion smashes a large screen in defiance of "Big Brother," an allusion to George Orwell's novel *1984*, and IBM, their chief competitor at the time.[2] While at Apple, Bill's leadership and coaching skills brought him multiple opportunities. After several roles within Apple, Bill became the CEO of Intuit. He served there from 1994 to 2000.

After an amazing career serving some of the most recognized brands in the world, you might think Campbell would head to the beach to enjoy his retirement. That's not exactly what he did.

For his final act, Bill joined the venture capital firm of Kleiner Perkins as an Executive in Residence. In essence, he would be a coach to many of the start-ups the company was backing. It was in this role that he earned his nickname as the trillion-dollar coach.[3] This final chapter of his illustrious career is really what earned Campbell a spot in this chapter.

Bill Campbell's impact cannot be captured in a single story, but it can be illustrated by the time he spent with Google. He served as the management team's coach, working 1:1 with every single Google executive, including Larry Page and Sergey Brin, who credit Bill with nearly all their success as a team.[4] Without him, Google may have never become the organization it is today.

For over twenty years, from their first days as a quirky start-up to one of the most valuable companies in the world, Bill was present through it all, coaching and meeting with each of the leaders weekly to ensure the holistic health of their high-performing team and keep them focused on the task at hand. What made Bill so valuable was his approach to developing leaders.

Most executive coaches at the time were developing people with a cookie cutter approach. Bill took a different path. Scott Cook, cofounder and then CEO of Intuit, recounted Bill's abilities, stating, "He appreciated that each person had a different story and background. He was so nuanced and different in how he approached growth challenges and leadership issues. Bill was a technicolor rainbow." His personalized approach, investing time in getting to know each person, was instrumental in his success . . . especially when the company was moving forward with their IPO.[5]

"Bill Campbell was a coach of teams. He built them, shaped them, put the right players in the right positions (and removed the wrong players from wrong positions), cheered them on, and kicked them in their collective butt when they were underperforming."[6] His role at Google is just one of the many examples in which Bill helped people get over their biggest hurdles and achieve greatness.

So, what did Bill actually teach people that made him a beloved, trusted, and iconic figure? His impact was so profound that, after his death, some of his protégés decided to write a book about what they had learned from him. In *Trillion Dollar Coach*, the authors share the leadership playbook they experienced under Bill's tutelage. The team interviewed eighty people who had been impacted by Bill's leadership and coaching. I know it's audacious to attempt to summarize someone else's leadership philosophy, so I won't go there. Bill did it for us. Here is the manifesto he wrote while the CEO of Intuit:[7]

It's the People

People are the foundation of any company's success. The primary job of each manager (leader) is to help people be more effective in their job and to grow and develop. We have great people who want to do well, and are capable of doing great things, and come to work fired up to do them. Great people flourish in an environment that liberates and amplifies that energy. Managers create this environment through support, respect, and trust.

Support means giving people the tools, information, training, and coaching they need to succeed. It means continuous effort to develop people's skills. Great managers help people excel and grow.

Respect means understanding people's unique career goals and being sensitive to their life choices. It means helping people achieve these career goals in a way that's consistent with the needs of the company.

Trust means freeing people to do their jobs and to make

decisions. It means knowing people want to do well and believing that they will.

What made Bill Campbell tick? I really don't know, but here's a clue. When he was transitioning the CEO role at Intuit to Brad Smith, he told Brad that he would go to bed every night thinking about the eight thousand souls who worked for him. "What are they thinking and feeling? How can I make them the best they can be?"[8]

Bill Campbell loved people, and they loved him back. It is so much easier to lead people if you love them. Do you really care about them as human beings? Do you want them to be successful in life and not just at work? You may think love is a high bar, and it is. However, if you consider the alternative, a world in which people are tolerated as opposed to being treasured, you can quickly see how that story ends.

In these situations, where people are viewed as cogs in the machine—as interchangeable parts—the people know this, they feel it. Leaders who lead with this worldview may wonder what happened to engagement and performance. It went out the window along with people's creativity, discretionary effort, and loyalty.

ENGAGE AND DEVELOP OTHERS

I was excited when I heard Bill Campbell's story. The more we researched, the more our team became convinced that at the core of his philosophy was the concept of Engage and Develop Others. This Fundamental worked for Bill and the scores of organizations he served, and it will work for you. This approach to leading people is packed with truth and value for every leader. Let's begin by exploring what it means to engage someone. You should think about this at two levels.

The first level is who you decide to engage or enlist to join your team. This is a nontrivial question. According to Peter Drucker, the most important decision a leader makes is "who does what." I agree with Drucker! The right people are essential to create a High Performance Team or organization.

Beyond Drucker's proclamation, there are many indicators pointing to the conclusion that the team with the best players has a greater chance of winning. Although this data is often muddy and the conclusions elusive, I think professional sports may provide a window into the linkage between level of talent and overall performance. Let's look at independent studies from Major League Baseball (MLB), the National Basketball Association (NBA), and the top leagues in European soccer.

- In MLB, a study by FiveThirtyEight found that from 1998 to 2019, the top-spending teams won about 55 percent of their games, while the bottom-spending teams won about 45 percent of their games.[9]
- According to a study by Duke University, NBA teams investing above the league average for player salaries have won fifteen of the last twenty-one championships.[10]
- In another study covering twenty seasons, the same pattern emerges in the world of elite football (soccer) clubs. The "Top 6" members of the English Premier League, made up of Manchester City, Manchester United, Liverpool, Chelsea, Tottenham, and Arsenal, consistently spend more than other clubs in the league. Since 2000,

twenty out of twenty-one championships have been won by a member of this group of six.[11]

I want to call out the fact that many other factors go into building a winning team beyond talent. There are clearly examples in which a big investment in talent has yielded disastrous results. However, this does not diminish the overarching theme: over time, if you accept the correlation between payroll and level of talent, better players yield more wins. When you think about who you will invite to join your team, aim high.

The next level of engagement is determined by what you do to ensure the talent you have already invited to join your team stays motivated to contribute at a high level. Ken Blanchard, the legendary leadership thought leader and my mentor for many years, says that everyone is an enthusiastic beginner on Day One. As it relates to engagement, a real test of leadership is how engaged these people are at the six-month and the six-year mark in their careers . . . and beyond.

Engagement, or the lack thereof, is one of the biggest challenges faced by organizations around the world. Tragically, many leaders are unaware of the dire state of their workforce. Gallup has been studying engagement and its impact on our organizations for decades. Globally, the number of employees who are fully engaged at work is staggeringly low, only 23 percent.[12] On the flip side, the organizations who have made engagement a priority produce unbelievable results. High-engagement workplaces yield 81 percent less absenteeism, 64 percent fewer safety incidents, 41 percent better quality, 28 percent less shrinkage (theft), and 23 percent more profitability![13] Leaders create the conditions that determine engagement.

Only organizations with engaged team members excel over the long haul.

The final facet of this Fundamental is the development of those we lead. What are we doing to help every individual in our organization grow? Is growth optional? Is it viewed as extracurricular?

My belief is we can never let personal growth become a "nice-to-do" activity. If we think we are too busy or don't need to grow, these attitudes can easily metastasize into the cancer of complacency, hubris, or irrelevance. Leaders must commit to lifelong learning and rally their entire organization to do the same. Arie de Gaus led the strategic planning group for Royal Dutch Shell. He said, "The ability to learn faster than your competition may be the only sustainable competitive advantage."[14]

The single best thing a leader can do if they want to add value over the entirety of a career is to commit to lifelong learning—not an intellectual ascent but a real commitment. What would it take for you to make learning a lifestyle, not a strategy or a list of activities? Your capacity to grow will determine your capacity to lead.

I know I just devoted a couple of paragraphs to *your* growth and development as a leader—that's not what this Fundamental is really about. It is about helping *others* grow. So why did I choose to start with you? Two reasons: People always watch the leader! That's the first reason. You will not have the moral authority to ask others to invest in personal development if you don't invest in your own. Second, if you keep growing, you'll be in a much better position to help your team grow. You are their coach and leader. Helping people grow is a big part of your role. Don't allow yourself to become stale or stagnant. Growing leaders grow organizations.

A BUSINESS OF BUSINESSPEOPLE

Our team had traveled to Springfield, Missouri—a long way from Bill Campbell and his Silicon Valley friends. The work we were about to encounter made the distance feel even farther than the 1,500 miles that separated us. We had arrived for a visit to Springfield Remanufacturing Corp. (SRC), whose core business at the time was rebuilding all types of engines.

While many Silicon Valley companies were focused on search engines, the team we were there to see was clearly focused on very different engines. Their products were used by numerous industries including agriculture, automotive, trucking, marine, and more. Yet, despite all the differences, I had the very real sense we were going to experience something extraordinary. We would not be disappointed.

We were there to meet Jack Stack, CEO, and see firsthand how he and his team had saved SRC from the brink of disaster. The company stock was ten cents a share when Jack and several of his coworkers decided to buy the company to prevent the parent company, International Harvester, from closing the facility. By their own admission, the new owners knew nothing about running a company. But they knew the clock was ticking and the turnaround needed to begin immediately. Their strategy was built on a hunch: a business of businesspeople will always outperform a business of employees.[15]

Turning employees into businesspeople became their highest priority. Under Jack's leadership, the team did several things. They began sharing the company financial statements with all employees. There were weekly meetings to talk about the financials and how to improve them in the next week. The role of the accountants was reframed. As Jack described the conversation, he acknowledged that they were outstanding when it came to telling us what happened in the past—they were serving as historians. He challenged them to instead become teachers, helping everyone at the company understand how to proactively have a positive impact on the numbers.

This probably sounds good and relatively simple, but to see it in reality was compelling. While we were visiting the plant, we looked into their backyard. It was littered with old, dead engines; many were covered in rust, and all looked to be a mere shadow of their prior selves. Most appeared to have parts missing, although I know very little about engines. You could just tell; these engines were in extreme disrepair. There was one guy outside working on an engine. We learned he was dismantling it. The parts would be cleaned and salvaged if possible, and new parts would be added to replace missing or irreparable ones. I was intrigued by the labor intensiveness of it all.[16]

Then our host explained that the yard is where most employees start their careers. He shared that many of the people who come into this role have no formal education beyond high school and some of them didn't make it to graduation. What he said next was the kicker. "On their first or second day on the job, we give them a full set of our financials. We tell them there will be a meeting on Friday for them to ask questions. We tell them their job is not really breaking down engines; their job is to improve the financial performance of the organization."[17]

Since my visit to SRC, Jack and his team have become famous in some circles; there have been a couple of books written about their accomplishments, and they have started many subsidiaries. SRC now does logistics, warehousing, fulfillment, trucking, and more.

I talked to Jack and a few of his leaders recently. He told me the reason they started the other businesses was because they had raised up so many talented business leaders, they didn't know what to do with them. For him, starting businesses was a way to steward the excess leadership they had created. Have you ever created so much leadership talent that you felt compelled to start new businesses as a release valve? In our recent survey, 58 percent of leaders globally say they don't have enough leaders for the future. Maybe you could take a page out of SRC's playbook.

Wouldn't it be costly to develop all those people? Well, it will cost something, but I would encourage you not to focus on the cost as much as on the return. Here's how that math has worked out for Jack over the last thirty years: SRC's stock price increased 348,000 percent. One thousand dollars invested in Berkshire Hathaway in 1983 would have been worth $113,000 in 2013; the same amount invested in SRC would have been worth $3.4 million. I guess it is true: a "business of businesspeople" will outperform a business of employees.[18]

STAND AND DELIVER

In 1993, the asteroid 5095 was officially dubbed Escalante. The man behind this honor was Bolivian American educator Jaime Alfonso Escalante Gutiérrez.

As a young teacher, Jaime decided that he would adopt a new style of teaching, a method that would make the content more engaging and exciting. He explains,

In 1952, while still an undergraduate in La Paz, Bolivia, I began teaching mathematics and physics—first at one high school, then a second, and finally a third. Early in my career I found that children learn faster when learning is fun, when it is a game and a challenge. From the beginning I cast the teacher in the role of "coach" and students in the role of the "team." I made sure that my students knew that we were all working together on the same team. In La Paz in the fifties and early sixties, our "opponent" was the annual secondary school mathematics competition. Our goal: to reign as the champions over all the local schools.[19]

Escalante moved to Los Angles and began teaching at Garfield High School in 1974. Just after he arrived, the school's accreditation was in jeopardy. The decision was made to increase their Advanced Placement offerings, and Escalante decided to teach calculus. At first, the kids and the administration were skeptical. However, he promised the kids if they learned math, they would be able to get jobs in engineering and technology.[20]

Escalante leveraged the AP exam, repositioning the test as a short-term, tangible goal that the students could rally around. He said this in his book:[21]

Few students today have not been lectured on the necessity and importance of a good education, but the dictum "Get a good education" may be too nebulous for easily distracted young minds. Their focus easily shifts to other more pressing problems, particularly when they are living in poverty. The AP test provides a formidable opponent that galvanizes each of the students and their teacher in a united charge toward a tangible and inexorable deadline: the second week of May.

In the beginning, acceptance of Escalante's ideas was low. In 1978, only five students took the AP exam but two passed. Here's how the next few years looked:[22]

1981—Fifteen students took the exam and fourteen passed.

1983—Thirty-three took the exam and thirty passed.

1990—Four-hundred-plus students were in Escalante's classes.

1991—Five hundred seventy students took the AP test.

On the surface, this decade looks like nothing but progress. This was not the case. As the results improved, so did the challenges. Even the administration threatened to fire Escalante because he came to the school too early and stayed too late. There were many obstacles, including death threats. What? Death threats for a teacher changing the lives of students through mathematics? Yes. Make a note, the pursuit of Uncommon Greatness will always encounter opposition.

The students and the world were the losers in the final chapter of this story. Tragically, Escalante left the school in 1991. After his departure, the number of students passing the calculus exam plummeted by 80 percent.[23]

The good news: more and more people have been inspired by Escalante's story. President Reagan awarded him the Medal of Excellence in Education. Jay Mathews wrote a book about his

life and work entitled *The Best Teacher in America*, and Holly-
wood made a feature film in 1988, *Stand and Deliver*.[24, 25]

––––––––––

As we conclude this chapter, I hope you are inspired by the stories of Campbell, Stack, and Escalante. Each of these men remind me of the power and responsibility we have as leaders to
steward the engagement and development of the people we serve.
In many situations, we will have others who can help—training
professionals, human resources staff, even outside partners like
coaches and mentors. All of this is fantastic. However, we can
never lose sight of our role.

With those we directly supervise, we need to coach, encourage,
challenge, resource, and provide the gift of accountability. For those
beyond our direct responsibility, we should always be a champion
for the people and their growth, development, and full engagement.
When we do these things consistently over time, everyone wins.

Try This: At a future meeting with your team, brain-
storm potential advantages you might expect if you were
to significantly increase the time, energy, effort, and resources you invest on this Fundamental. What might
happen if you were serious about Engaging and Developing the people in your organization?

For access to the FREE Uncommon Greatness digital self-assessment and help with your next steps, text
uncommon to 66866 or scan the QR code in the Resources section at the end of the book.

ENGAGE AND DEVELOP OTHERS: IDEAS FOR ACTION

I f you've read any of my recent work, you know I am a huge fan of Peter Drucker. The late management and leadership guru is one of my heroes. His level of clarity on most topics was refreshing. As it relates to the final test of a leader, he said, "Do they produce results, and do they have followers?" When we Engage and Develop Others, we make both of these outcomes much more likely.

In this chapter we'll explore several strategies and some supporting tactics to help you pass Drucker's test. Specifically, we'll do a deep dive on **Build Trust**, **Help People Grow**, **Build Genuine Community**, and **Cast Dynamic Vision**.

BUILD TRUST

Every leader wants and needs trust. The challenge: trust is earned. As leaders, we must engage in the activities that engender trust.

If we don't, we may end up with compliant followers rather than committed ones. The difference between the two is hard for me to express because the chasm is so immense. Here's the best I have in the moment: compliance is the seedbed for mediocrity, and commitment is the fuel for sustained levels of elite performance. Let's Build Trust! The following paragraphs contain ideas that work.

Create Safety. How safe is your workplace? The first thing that comes to mind for me when I hear that question is the level of physical safety and security. This is critically important. But another facet of safety is how your people feel.

Have you created a place where everyone feels empowered and even encouraged to contribute? Google did some research a few years back to determine why some of their teams outperformed others. They called the project Aristotle, a nod to his comment about the "whole is greater than the sum of its parts." What they discovered is that in the best teams, the leader had created psychological safety. Yet, the question remained: How do you create this condition?[1]

First, focus on problems, not people. Every time you and your team go into problem-solving mode, you have a choice to make: Will you focus on the problem or the people? Yes, there are almost always people involved. However, if you focus on the process and the problems, you will create more psychological safety. This does not mean you should not hold people accountable. In fact, one of my favorite practices is to end every discussion with the following question: Who will do what by when?

Next, the Google team discovered the importance of good facilitation. As it turns out, this underrated skill is one of the most important elements in team and organizational effectiveness.

Think of a facilitator as someone who is designated to remove barriers. This happens in two ways.

One, they anticipate and remove barriers before they manifest. For example, having the right people in the room and ensuring necessary pre-work goes out in advance.

Next, the facilitator identifies barriers in real time and addresses them. If you agree that it's important to hear from everyone on important matters, a good facilitator will notice when someone is not contributing. "Gigi, we haven't heard from you on this issue. What are you thinking?" Or they will notice when someone is making the conversation too personal. "Hold on, Sam. That sounds personal. Let's take the personalities out of this for now. Try that again and tell us what you think the root problem is." A great facilitator is a steward of psychological safety.

Watch Your Words. Words matter. You know this. However, if we are not vigilant, our conversations can drift from positive to punitive. This all begins with your language. Are your words generally constructive or critical? Are they encouraging or corrosive? What you say carries a lot of weight. The language you allow in your organization matters.

I was introduced to the concept of Killer Phrases decades ago. The best I can remember, it was Chic Thompson[2] who raised this red flag for me. However, after I became aware of the concept, I picked up phrases to guard against from Joyce Weiss, J. Sullivan, Jill Purdy, and others. Here are some things you may be saying, or allowing others to say, that are killing psychological safety (and stifling creativity) in your organization.

Yes, but . . .
We tried that before.

Who did this?
That will never work.
It'll never fly.
Have you lost your mind?
Our technology won't support that.
That's fine in theory . . .
The boss will kill that.
Who's going to pay for that?
Are you kidding me?
That's not in the budget.
Is that your best idea?
Okay, it's your career.

Be on the lookout for the phrases above and any others that you believe are impeding trust, innovation, and risk-taking in your organization, starting with your own language. You can even ask your team if there are any things you say repeatedly that communicate your deeper feelings of doubt, skepticism, and judgment. Ban all Killer Phrases from your organization and you'll create more collaboration, creativity, and trust.

Trust Others. To create more trust in the workplace, leaders must trust people. I know this may sound obvious, but it matters. Now, I know I said earlier that trust must be earned. So, I'm not suggesting you should lose your mind and trust everyone with everything. Competency matters. Context matters. Consequences matter too. However, I want to use this as a moment to challenge you again on your role as a leader.

Managers want to control people, and leaders want to empower and release them. There is a fundamental difference. Managers typically want to treat each person the same; leaders treat them differently. You want to lead. Manage systems, processes, and budgets—lead people.

A key element of leadership is the work you empower and enable others to do. I have had too many conversations with people in positions of leadership who want to control everything; most feel this is necessary to ensure the desired outcome. This is not a sign of their leadership prowess; it is a sign of their lack of leadership.

If you, as the leader, must micromanage all the work under your responsibility, I know at least one thing about you: you have created a real and tangible cap to what you can accomplish due to personal capacity limits. If you want to expand your leadership capacity, you will have to create the conditions necessary for you to trust people.

HELP PEOPLE GROW

Growing leaders grow organizations. Helping people grow increases individual contribution, engagement, and performance. Although I believe individuals must ultimately accept the responsibility for their own personal and professional growth, I think leaders have a significant role to play. Here are a few ideas to help you get started (or continue) on this path.

Champion Growth. If we want to really Help People Grow, we must meet them where they are. We must champion growth. I am not against formal training that attempts to inculcate a common language, approach, or best practices within an organization. I have long been an advocate for organizations to establish a core curriculum required for all. However, this strategy will ultimately prove helpful but inadequate.

I'm a huge fan of individual support when it comes to helping people grow. Why provide individual support? There is probably a long list of reasons. Here are a few of them.

People have different learning styles. What's your primary learning style? Do you know the way members of your team learn best? You should know. If someone learns best in a relational context, be sure they have a coach or mentor to spur their growth. If they prefer books, give them a reading list. If they are an experiential learner, give them a project to accelerate their learning.

People have different career objectives. If someone wants to advance as far and as fast as they can in your organization, and you believe they have significant untapped potential, you will likely create a different and more rigorous growth plan for them than you would the person whose career aspiration is to do their job well and nothing more. We can often see more in a person than they can see themselves, but we cannot establish their career aspirations. I have encountered numerous people in my career who chose to serve well below their capabilities—ultimately, this is their choice to make.

I don't want to miss this opportunity to serve. One of the greatest sources of joy for me is to help someone grow. I know this is selfish and may not be part of your motivation, but intellectual integrity demanded this be on *my* list. I love it when I can help someone live, lead, or work at a higher level. If you have not experienced this sensation, you can. I think you'll find it to be an extremely fulfilling part of your role as a leader.

Recognize Growth. One of the things I have written about over the years is the power of recognition. The earliest source I can find advocating the power of recognition is from Plato in the year 375 BCE. He said, "What is honored in a country will be cultivated there."[3]

If you want more growth-oriented behaviors in your organization, honor those behaviors; recognize growth. This can be done publicly or privately—preferably both. Recognize not just the outcome, such as the degree bestowed or the certificate earned, but also honor the effort, diligence, and tenacity to pursue that goal.

Who are the heroes in your organization? You can probably identify multiple categories, from top performers to the innovators and maybe even those with long tenure. These are all outstanding! Have you ever considered making those who demonstrate curiosity, lifelong learning, and a growth mindset an additional group of heroes?

Here's a cautionary note about recognizing growth. As much of your recognition as possible needs to be personalized. I know that sounds like a lot of work, and it is. Remember, managers want to treat everyone the same, but leaders do not. Why would I advocate this seemingly extreme idea?

People are different. Some people would rather not be singled out publicly for their accomplishments. Some would prefer a heartfelt word from you in private. Others would be more excited about a handwritten note, something they could read over and over again. Still others would just as soon have a trophy or a plaque to display, and some would be most excited if you gave them a bonus or a day off. Remember the reason you are recognizing the growth in the first place. You are attempting to honor the person and the behavior. If your recognition is not honoring in the eyes of the individual, you missed a real opportunity.

Meet with members of your team and ask them to tell you

about the best recognitions they ever received. I've done this with a lot of people over the years. You will be amazed at the diversity of the responses. Take good notes on what you learn.

Provide Resources. Regardless of a person's preferred learning style, everyone can benefit from the right resource at the right time. This may appear to be a topic that needs very little explanation. Of course, leaders provide resources. Not so fast. First, we need to examine the term. What constitutes a resource?

To you a resource may be a book or an article. Not a bad guess, but this is a very limited view. What if the resource the person needs is an outside coach or a mentor? What if the resource they need is a membership to an association where they can have access to industry best practices? What if this person is a networker and learns best from experiences—will you approve their request to attend a conference, or two, or three? What if this person desires more formal education? Can you and the organization help with tuition expenses?

I'm not suggesting you have to do all of these things. Just be careful not to assume the individual will figure it all out on their own. In an ideal world, you want the person to shoulder the bulk of the responsibility for their growth and development, but I believe the organization can help lighten the load.

Meet with members of your team. Reiterate your desire to help them grow both personally and professionally. Ask them what resources they believe would be most helpful to them at this stage of their career. See what you can do to help.

Here's a quick disclaimer to the language I just used regarding "personally and professionally." I always think a leader's first priority when we attempt to Help People Grow is to first help them close any critical gaps that may exist. Many years ago, I was leading a team of consultants. One of them made the case for why he should learn a foreign language. There was some merit to his rationale. However, he was a consultant, and his skills were underdeveloped and his performance lagging. So, in this situation, we decided it best to invest our limited resources and his limited time on consulting resources.

BUILD GENUINE COMMUNITY

About thirty years ago, our team began a decades-long exploration of the topic of high performance that continues today. Prior to that time, we had always been a fan of teams and individuals who excelled at their chosen craft. However, being starstruck is not the same as being a serious student of these outliers. This all changed in the late 1980s with our attempts to understand the world of teams. We knew the vast majority of teams in the world were mediocre while another large group were just awful—the chronic underperformers. Both of these groups were interesting but not helpful. We decided to study the best of the best. We ultimately called these High Performance Teams.

Almost two decades into that exploration, I shared our conclusions in *The Secret of Teams*. The reason that is relevant here is that these elite, High Performance Teams have one trait that differentiates them from all the rest: Community. A deep and abiding sense of belonging held by members of the group. When an organization can understand and apply this across the enterprise, there is nothing more powerful to raise the engagement and ultimately the performance of their organization. Community is the turbocharger and the difference maker, separating the good teams from the great ones. There are several things you can do to build community.

Set the Strategy. I remember the day I had the opportunity to sit with Jon Katzenbach, co-author of *The Wisdom of Teams*. Our team had been working on our research regarding teams for many years, and Jon and I had reached very different conclusions about the odds of a team becoming great.

In his book, Jon said the odds of an individual being part of a great team was about once in a career. He defended his position by saying that the likelihood of a team caring deeply about each other was a real rarity. In his mind, it was this deep and genuine level of care that enabled good teams to become great ones. His final word—don't count on it.[4]

As I foreshadowed in the earlier paragraph, our team had reached a similar conclusion regarding the importance of care and concern among a team. As Jon and I talked, I first listened intently and affirmed his findings on the importance of this intangible. I told him we called what he was describing community. Then, as diplomatically as possible, I told him that rather than see it as a once-in-a-career phenomenon, I believed that if the leader committed to the strategy of building community, they could make it happen more than 90 percent of the time.

The key, I said, is the leader. Yes, if left to chance, the odds could be once in a career. Neither people nor teams drift to greatness; they drift to mediocrity, or worse. But if the leader embraces building genuine community as part of their strategy and leads in the execution of that strategy, it will work with amazing consistency.

Jon was gracious and said our premise might explain

something he had experienced after writing the book. He said he had begun to notice more and more teams who seemed to be beating the odds and creating what we called "community." Now he said he understood how they were doing it.

If you want to create genuine community, the first step is for you to decide that you are committed to building it and then set the strategy.

Value Diversity. Diversity has become a hot topic in recent years and rightly so. There are many reasons this is a welcomed shift in our social consciousness. Besides being the right thing to do, the business case is clear.

- In 2018, Gartner research revealed that inclusive teams unlock diversity benefits by improving team performance by up to 30 percent in high diversity environments.[5]
- In 2020, Glassdoor reported 76 percent of job seekers said a diverse workforce was an important factor in their decision.[6]

Although the value of diversity is now making headlines, it is not a new idea. In *The Medici Effect,* Frans Johansson points out that one of the leading factors that gave rise to the explosion of innovation, creativity, scientific discovery, and artistic expression that we now call the Renaissance was the diversity of the people who assembled in the region around Florence, Italy, in the late fourteenth century.[7]

I have been challenging people on the topic of diversity for decades. However, my example is not as historically rich as the Renaissance. I typically talk about baseball. Imagine you had a baseball team with nine second basemen. What do you think would happen? Who would pitch? Who would catch? You might be able to field a team, but I have no doubt their performance would be awful. Recruit, select, develop, promote, and celebrate diversity, and your team will win more games.

If diversity is an opportunity area for you, consider the following tactics.

- Broaden Your Definition—Diversity represents richness. Be sure you are not defining it too narrowly. Think about differing perspectives, experience, background, education, ethnicity, race, religion, personality, and more.
- Recruit Widely—Look for ways to expand your network. A good way to find diverse candidates is to look in places you've not previously explored. When Satya Nadella became CEO of Microsoft, the organization moved from recruiting at only sixteen universities to more than five hundred.[8]
- Screen People In—This is another idea I picked up from Microsoft. Under Nadella's leadership they moved from trying to screen people out to screening them in. They now consciously look for ways a candidate could potentially add value rather than focusing on the reasons not to select them.
- Honor All Voices—I have tried for decades to build diverse teams in the broadest sense possible—age, ethnicity, gender, background, education, experience, and more. However, the Google project Aristotle I mentioned earlier found that diversity alone did not matter, unless these diverse people contribute freely. On the best teams, everyone contributes. The conversations are not

dominated by a few. Even when I have led diverse teams, I have not always done a great job of ensuring equal participation. My rationale has been that some people prefer not to share on some issues. In retrospect, our teams lost a tremendous amount of valuable input. For the best work, you need to honor *all* voices.

Know Others Deeply. Although I am not aware of a universally agreed-upon definition of community in the context I am describing, I believe the cornerstone of community is always a deep understanding of the other members of your group. For many years, I have included "a place where people know and are known" in my working definition of community. Leaders must promote knowing others deeply. If you do not, the normal course of life will make this process take many months or even years. And, without your involvement, it may not happen at all. A few things about this aspect of community.

Knowing and being known is cumulative over time. I am currently part of a group that has been meeting every two weeks for over twenty-five years. We've missed a few weeks but not many. We continue to learn more and more about each other, both during our meetings and in our interactions between sessions. As we do, our community is deepened and strengthened.

Allow people to move at their own pace. Although an individual may willingly join the community, individual comfort levels will vary, as will the pace of assimilation. There will be a period of testing. Is this really a safe place? Will I be judged if I tell the truth about my life or circumstances? What are the boundaries and norms of this group? Are confidential things held in confidence? As these questions and others like them are answered, a person will gradually become part of the community.

You can only invite someone into community—you cannot force them. Community is a unique gift; it can be offered but the individual must receive it as a full participant. There are no bystanders in genuine community.

Pick one of the groups you participate in on a regular basis, perhaps your team. Try an experiment. Ask a "know and being known question" at your next meeting. Don't make it too threatening (e.g., I would not ask, "What is your greatest fear about the future?"). Try something much easier, such as, "What is your favorite food and why?" Or, "What's your favorite movie and why?" I know these questions may feel trivial—they are. But remember, community is cumulative over time. As the weeks become months and the months become years, you can ask far more challenging questions.

Celebrate Often. Another hallmark of genuine community is the persistence of celebration. People in community are always looking for legitimate opportunities to celebrate the accomplishments of the group and the individuals within the group.

Here are a few tips to consider as you work to incorporate celebration into your team or organization.

- Don't Miss the Big Events—Weddings, college graduations, the birth of children, and anniversaries all count in my book as big events. Make your own list. What else would you include?
- Don't Miss the Small Events—There is a gold mine here waiting to be excavated. Too many groups miss the big stuff I just mentioned, but very few even acknowledge

the small stuff. Here are a few ideas to jump-start your creativity: accomplishments of the children of those in your group, project milestones, a new customer, acknowledging trips and other activities that take place outside of work. Maybe someone ran their first marathon or climbed a mountain—all good reasons to celebrate!

- Don't Overdo It—Celebrations don't need to be elaborate. Almost nothing is too small here. Mere acknowledgment is often sufficient. However, some judgment is required. If a team member just ran an ultramarathon, that might deserve more than a "Cool." In many cases, a few heartfelt words from you or others in the group will be enough to affirm the individual and the accomplishment.

How do you celebrate a life accomplishment or a personal milestone by a member of your group? Sometimes you just show up. When a member of my group has a death in the family, it is not uncommon for the majority of the guys to show up to celebrate a life and mourn together.

I remember a time I was in community with a guy who was excited about his son's first middle school football game. He had been talking about it for a long time—that was my clue that it was a big deal. When that Thursday afternoon in August rolled around, I was preparing to leave the office early to head to the game; in our town, they play those games right after school.

As I was leaving, someone asked me where I was going. I told them to a middle school football game. Their next question: "Is your son playing?" "No," I said. "But I have a dear friend whose son is playing in his first game. I want to be there to celebrate with him." I remember thinking, *I don't even know if the kid will get any playing time, but it doesn't matter. I want to be there to hug their necks and celebrate with them regardless.* That's just the kind of thing you do in community.

CAST DYNAMIC VISION

Why do people follow your leadership? There are probably several factors, but somewhere in the mix there is a sense of their personal alignment and resonance with the vision, mission, or purpose of your organization. Without this, you'll often find your connection with the people you lead reduced to a transactional relationship at best.

I spoke earlier about the desire for people to be committed as opposed to just complying with the minimal expectations of the job. I want every leader in the world to have the chance to lead people who believe in you and the cause you are pursuing. Once you move past your trustworthiness as a leader, the next biggest factor required to gain this level of buy-in is a vision people can believe in. Once you have it, here are some ideas on how to share it.

Say It Succinctly. Do you have a vision for your organization? Maybe you don't use that term. Maybe you call it mission, or purpose, or perhaps you have core values. I recently wrote about the importance of having some type of aspiration in *Culture Rules*. As I shared this idea with our entire organization at our annual event, I encouraged them to be sure their aspiration, regardless of language, is clear, simple, and repeatable.

I know I've quoted Peter Drucker a couple of times in the previous pages; as I confessed, I am a big fan of his clarity of thought and his insights on the topic of leadership decades before others were thinking about the topic with much rigor. Here's what he had to say about vision (aka mission statements): "The effective mission statement is short and sharply focused. It should fit on a t-shirt."[9]

Fit on a T-shirt! How's that for a standard? Your vision needs to be that clear, simple, and repeatable.

Ask ten people on your team, or better yet, from across your organization, what your organization's vision is (or whatever term you choose). They should all give you the same answer. In an ideal world, the language will be the same too. If the answers you get aren't what you would have hoped for, the problem might be lack of clarity or succinctness, or the source of the problem might be traceable to my next recommendation.

Say It Again. Human beings in the modern organization have a lot going on. From meetings, emails, and text messages to the actual work they have been charged to complete and the problems they encounter, all converge to create a blizzard for them to navigate on a daily basis. Add to this the out-of-office challenges—many have aging parents and some have children with ballet, sports, and the arts cramming every minute of their "free time." Combine all of this with the personal, administrative, and household duties such as car maintenance, banking matters, grocery shopping, meal prep, paying the bills, community involvement, serving on the school board, volunteering at the food bank, and so much more, and the modern life is more complex than at any point in history.

Enter a leader who wants to give you a higher purpose for the work you do on a daily basis. How in the world will this message break through?

Early in his academic career, John Kotter became the youngest tenured professor in Harvard's history; he was fascinated by organizational change. I met John after he took an early retirement and began his global consulting practice. Based on his research, he believes most organizations seeking to make a change under-communicate the needed messages to support the change by a factor of 10![10]

I respect John tremendously; however, I think he grossly underestimates the amount of communication needed to make large-scale change work. Most of the change efforts I have witnessed need one hundred times more airtime and energy than they receive. You must elevate the change—the vision, benefits, challenges, rationale, and support—above the noise of daily life. The inertia of the present is tremendous. Strategic and repetitive communications are an essential catalyst to keep the change in motion.

Leaders make the erroneous assumption that, when they say something, people will hear it, understand it, internalize it, and immediately act upon it. This is pure fantasy. The only way to break through the tsunami of information, distraction, clutter, and noise with your message is strategic repetition. You are going to have to say the most important things over and over and over again.

How many times did you talk about your vision in the last thirty days? Look back at your calendar to jog your memory. Let me challenge you to talk about the vision in some shape or form every day, multiple times a day. If you want people to get it, you're going to have to say it again and again.

Say It Differently. I do believe that leaders need to repeat the vision constantly. Unfortunately, that tactic alone will probably be insufficient to have your message permeate the heart and mind of everyone in your organization. You must learn to say it differently. Now, I don't just mean with different stories. While this approach will keep your message fresh and relevant, it still won't penetrate the life of everyone in your organization.

According to Howard Gardner's pioneering work on how people receive and process information, he has identified eight patterns or predispositions people have when they encounter information. He calls these our multiple intelligences. The reason this matters to me and you: as leaders, what is important is not *our* preferred style of communication; what's most critical is our audience's preferred method of receiving information. Here's where it gets tricky: every audience you address has a mix of many different intelligences. Therefore, odds are good that, without conscious effort on your part, much of what you say will fall on deaf ears. That's why, over time, you and I need to learn to communicate in as many of the intelligences as possible.

If this sounds rather abstract, let me illustrate with a very brief description and an example for each of Gardner's eight intelligences:[11]

1. **Linguistic**—This intelligence is represented in the people who love words—the written and spoken word. Writers, poets, and pastors likely have this intelligence in their mix.
2. **Mathematical**—These are the people who enjoy numbers. Engineers, physicists, and accountants are examples of people who probably have this intelligence.
3. **Intrapersonal**—Individuals who have this as a top intelligence are typically self-aware. These people can

gravitate to philosophy and psychology as their field of study.

4. **Interpersonal**—This group interacts well with others and understands both verbal and nonverbal communications. They learn and process information well during a conversation. Therapist and counselors often embody these attributes.

5. **Kinesthetic**—This intelligence is linked to our body— our sense of movement and control. Professional athletes, dancers, chiropractors, and people who enjoy physically interacting with a problem are in this group.

6. **Visual**—If you like to draw, sketch, paint, or sculpt, you may have this type of intelligence. People in this group learn better and faster if they can see a visual or a diagram of the concept you're attempting to communicate. Artists, architects, and designers typically showcase this intelligence.

7. **Musical**—As the name implies, these people speak the language of music. Often, they are composers, musicians, or disc jockeys.

8. **Naturalist**—Have you ever known a person who was happiest when they were outside? Maybe they had this as one of their leading intelligences. They typically like to learn via experiments. Many of these individuals have found their place in the sciences (e.g., geology, botany, zoology) or roles that allow them to work outside.

Think about an important upcoming message you need to deliver to your team or organization. Go back through the list of intelligences and see how many of them you can integrate into your strategy. Can you add additional stats for the math folks? Can you add a diagram to illustrate your big idea for the visual group? Your goal is to check as many of the boxes as you can. The more intelligences you employ, the more resonance and traction your message will get.

Over the last twenty-five years, many have asked which of the Fundamentals is most important. I think this could be a question with no right answer—all the Fundamentals are essential. However, to Engage and Develop Others may be the Fundamental that will require the most energy and personal attention over the course of your career. Although all the Fundamentals are "always on," none will require more of your daily focus than this one. Every conversation, meeting, and presentation represents an opportunity to demonstrate this Fundamental in action. People will be challenged, inspired, encouraged, and equipped by the things you say and do.

You can build a reputation as one of the elite leaders that makes everyone better. Sometimes these improvements will be the result of your direct interventions with individuals, and countless other times your impact will be indirect or intended for the masses. In either case, as you consciously work to Engage and Develop Others, you will grow not only the people around you; you will also grow yourself.

ENGAGE AND DEVELOP OTHERS
BEST PRACTICES AND KEY STRATEGIES

Build Trust
- Create Safety
- Watch Your Words
- Trust Others

Help People Grow
- Champion Growth
- Recognize Growth
- Provide Resources

Build Genuine Community
- Set the Strategy
- Value Diversity
- Know Others Deeply
- Celebrate Often

Cast Dynamic Vision
- Say It Succinctly
- Say It Again
- Say It Differently

Fundamental #3

REINVENT CONTINUOUSLY

ESCAPE THE NORM

*The arrogance of success is to think that what you
did yesterday will be sufficient for tomorrow.*

WILLIAM POLLARD

The essence of Reinvent Continuously is embodied in the work of a scientist—experimenting, tweaking the variables, and documenting the outcome, always with an intense focus on careful observation. All this effort is undertaken with one goal in mind: to discover the optimal path forward. This way of thinking is exactly what is required to create viral content on the internet.

In a world where trends can last as little as a few days, viral content either needs to be created and published incredibly quickly or it needs to be so compelling that it will capture the viewers' attention and imagination. In addition to the timing of the content, it must be new and fresh to keep that audience engaged or else you could lose them. Currently, one of the best in the world at creating this type of content is MrBeast.

Jimmy Donaldson, or MrBeast as he is known on YouTube, is a content creator, philanthropist, and entrepreneur. As of this writing, he has over 150 million subscribers on his main channel (over 251 million across all his channels). However, this number grossly understates his reach. His YouTube channels have recorded more than 37 billion views, with some individual videos that have been seen by more than 412 million people.[1] Donaldson has sights set on being the first person to have one billion followers on social media. MrBeast has certainly captured the imagination of a growing group of fans.

His videos are known for their creativity and wild stunts like "Squid Game in Real Life" and "Going Through the Same Drive Thru 1,000 Times," but that's not all.[2,3] With his newfound success, he has begun to focus on philanthropy: raising millions of dollars for charity, planting millions of trees, and giving away cars, houses, and money to people in need.

MrBeast's impact on YouTube and in the world has made him an important figure for many people, especially younger generations who look up to him as a role model for making a positive difference in the world.

But his was not some meteoric rise to fame and success. Donaldson began his journey at fourteen years old, with his original channel called MrBeast6000. In those early days, he would upload gaming content including *Minecraft*, *Pokémon Online*, and *Black Ops 2*. His first video to go viral was when he decided he would shock his viewers by counting to one hundred thousand in one sitting. It pulled in millions of views, and the rest is history.[4]

In 2016, Donaldson aimed to continue his success, but with a benevolent spin using "shock generosity." In these videos he gave cash away to those in need, and even recently he used his funds to create videos in which he helped one thousand people cure their blindness, paying for their procedures and documenting the process.[5]

In a world in which many of my posts receive very little attention, how is it possible for Donaldson to accomplish what he has? His success probably can't be reduced to any one single factor, unless perhaps it is his ability to practice our third Fundamental: Reinvent Continuously. Here are a few of the lessons leaders can learn from MrBeast as it relates to Reinvent Continuously.[6, 7, 8, 9]

Learn from Others. Before Jimmy began his YouTube career, he says he watched thousands of hours of YouTube content. He wanted to understand the internet wave. He was thirteen at the time.

More Ideas = Better Ideas. Jimmy believes the single most important element in his success are the ideas. He spends countless hours generating ideas, consistently carving out one hour each day, minimum, for solo idea generation sessions. This does not include the time he invests in brainstorming with his team.

Capture Your Ideas. Jimmy says he has over ten thousand ideas for future videos stored on his phone. How many ideas to improve the future have you captured?

Every Video Is an Opportunity to Improve. Jimmy says, "Fail often. Make one hundred videos and improve something every time."

Involve Others. Jimmy understands that being so close to his work, he can't be objective. Before he releases a video, he asks others to tear it apart and incorporates their feedback.

Be Patient. The process of reinventing his content and brand didn't happen overnight, nor did his success. After his first three years of producing content, MrBeast had only two thousand followers.

Consistently posting videos with tens of millions of views has made MrBeast a multimillion-dollar media company. His fame has garnered him other opportunities he may not have anticipated, such as being invited to Harvard to talk about his unique business model. He was also offered $1 billion for his brand. He said no.[10, 11]

Not only has Donaldson worked to reinvent his content and his approach to creating it, but he is also continuing to reinvent his business. In addition to his growing YouTube enterprise, MrBeast now has several branded products including chocolate bars, cookies, snack bars, an extensive merchandise line, and a burger chain with over 1,700 outlets that surpassed $100 million in revenue in 2022.[12, 13]

Donaldson has totally embraced the idea of Reinventing Continuously. He believes he must change to ultimately reach his goal of being the best content provider on the internet. To achieve and sustain a grand vision always requires reinvention. I can hardly wait to see what MrBeast comes up with next.

REINVENT CONTINUOUSLY

Most leaders understand the need for reinvention. The idea that you could continue to do what you've always done, the way you've always done it, and expect that to work indefinitely is crazy. So, if the concept is not foreign to leaders, what's the rub? Why do so many leaders appear reluctant to change? I think what some leaders appear to be missing is the frequency and

velocity of change required in today's world. This Fundamental
is always in motion, always in play . . . continuously!

But what does it mean to reinvent? It means to hold the processes, procedures, methods, and mindsets of the past with respect, not reverence. You must be willing to escape the grip of
your past and current practices, even your successes, before you
can take a fresh look at the possibilities of the future. This posture
allows you to proactively and strategically pursue improvement.

There are three primary domains where you should always
be looking for opportunities to reinvent: self, systems, and
structure.

Self—This domain is about you. If you are not learning, growing, and improving, it will be extremely difficult for you to
muster the moral authority to inspire those around you to do
so. People always watch the leader. Where do you begin? Any-
where you would like; remember, you have the rest of your life
to reinvent yourself. Here are some questions to stimulate your
self-assessment.

- Do you currently have any critical skill gaps that are
  significantly limiting your effectiveness in your current
  role? Are you sure? Who could you ask that cares enough
  to tell you the truth? What might happen if you closed
  a critical gap?
- What do you need to do to prepare for your next opportunity? Which skills will you likely need for a future role
  that you don't have today? Imagine your successful self
  a decade from now; what do you see? What do you need
  to do today to ensure that you become that future self?

- How would those who work with you describe you? If you weren't present, what would they say about you? What aspects of your leadership do others think you need to change? What's stopping you?
- How is your health? What could you do to make it better? I must ask, are you getting enough sleep? Exercise? How's your diet? When was your last physical? What would it take for you to move your health and well-being to the top of your priority list? A strong, healthy, well-rested you is a gift to those you lead.

Chances are high that no one is going to change you but you. You are the only one who can reinvent you. When it comes to you, as my friend Henry Cloud says, you are ridiculously in charge. Please don't forfeit your agency.

Systems—This domain refers to the way work is accomplished in your organization. My friend and mentor Randy Gravitt says it like this: "The systems, work processes, and behaviors in your organization are perfectly aligned to the outcomes you are currently obtaining."

Here's a thought: this principle applies far beyond the workplace . . .

The student who is not satisfied with her grades will likely need to change her study habits—or hire a tutor, or get more sleep, or whatever—if she wants a better grade.

The person who wants better relationships will likely need to communicate with people differently, invest more time, or become a better listener.

The individual who wants more financial freedom will need

to either earn more, spend less, save and invest differently, or perhaps do a combination of all of these.

Even the gardener who wants more and better tomatoes needs to do something differently—perhaps plant different seeds, switch soils, use fertilizer, water more or less, place the plants in more sun or more shade. If you really want better tomatoes, you need to make a change to what you're currently doing.

The concept is the same for every leader who wants different outcomes.

I've been talking about this idea for decades. Unfortunately, too many leaders are simply hoping for different outcomes. Hope is not a strategy for improvement. What are you willing to change in search of different outcomes? What are you willing to reinvent?

Structure—Of the three domains we're reviewing here, I find this to be most often overlooked or undervalued. Too many leaders play the role of victim when it comes to structure. I should quickly say I understand that the vast majority of leaders do not control the structure of their organizations. Ultimately, the CEO and board are the only ones who have the final say on major, overarching decisions regarding structure. However, don't miss the structural elements within your control.

How will your team, department, or division organize to do work? What about the cross-functional team you just launched? You have influence, if not the decision, on the committee and the ad hoc project team you just launched—how will they be structured?

I know some of you are hoping this paragraph or the next will answer the question: How should these groups of people be organized? I don't know. Here's what I do know: structure should enable, not inhibit, the accomplishment of the task at hand. Here are a few questions to help you decide if you need to reinvent your structure.

- Does it feel like we are spinning our wheels?
- Is it becoming harder and harder to accomplish the work?
- Do we have the right people involved to make decisions and advance the work?
- Are things falling through the cracks?
- Is the final work routinely late or over budget?

Here's the deal with structure, regardless of the answers to the previous questions: there is no guarantee structure is the problem. In many cases, the root problem can be found in the domains of self or systems and, sometimes, the problem's roots can be traced to one of the other Fundamentals. However, if you don't like your answers to any of these questions, ask yourself, *Is our structure helping us accomplish our desired outcomes, or is it hindering us?* From time to time, you will need to reinvent your structure.

If you will Reinvent Continuously, you create the best odds for your long-term relevance, vitality, and contribution as a leader. You are uniquely positioned to be the architect of the future. To step up and fulfill your calling, you must Reinvent Continuously.

TIME FOR A CHANGE

In 2007, Arianna Huffington was having the time of her life, or so it appeared. To the world, she was a successful mother, journalist, CEO, entrepreneur, and more. She had cofounded the *Huffington Post* and changed the media landscape forever. Her internet-based news outlet was the first major agency to incorporate user-generated content. She also had tremendous influence on how people consume content online. In 2006, Huffington was named as one of the one hundred most influential people in the world by *Time* magazine, and she was also an advocate for the environment. Arianna was a star in many universes. What was unknown to most was the terrible price she was paying for her accomplishments.[14]

After working late into the night in preparation for her organization's coverage of the 2008 presidential election, Huffington collapsed in her home office in Los Angeles. When she fell, she struck her face on her desk, breaking her cheekbone. The diagnosis: exhaustion. By her own admission, Huffington had been misguided by the popular misconception that sleep deprivation was a badge of honor. During her recovery, she came to grips with the fact her lifestyle needed to change—starting with her sleep habits.[15]

In her book *The Sleep Revolution*, Huffington describes herself as a sleep evangelist. She makes a strong case for why every leader should consider reinventing their sleep habits—in the process, you may find you've reinvented your life and leadership as well.

Huffington is not the only leader to see this global, silent pandemic unfolding before our wide-open eyes.

- The Manchester United Football Club built a two-hundred-million-euro facility with eighty sleeping rooms for the team to use before every home game. They are serious about controlling the total sleep experience, not just the duration.[16]

- The Seattle Seahawks now have assigned sleep coaches and are using sleep tracking devices to monitor and adjust each player's sleep routine.[17]
- A Gallup study found 40 percent of Americans are clinically sleep-deprived, while 70 percent admit they aren't getting enough sleep.[18]
- A UK study found that sleep-deprived people are seven times more likely to feel helplessness and five times more likely to feel lonely.[19]
- Lack of sleep has been linked to *seven of the top fifteen* leading causes of death in the United States—our lack of sleep is literally killing us.[20]

As I believe Huffington would testify, often, the most profound work we can do as leaders is focused on ourselves. However, I understand that, for many of you, your greatest opportunity to reinvent yourself is not in the area of sleep. What is it? What do you need to reinvent about *you* to take your life and leadership to the next level? Your shot at Uncommon Greatness may hang in the balance.

KEEP PEDALING

When you think of reinvention, what comes to mind? For many, we envision the masterstroke or moment of insight like Archimedes's eureka moment. This is not Dave Brailsford's view of reinvention.

Born in Derbyshire, England, in 1964, Brailsford studied

sports science in his undergraduate education. This preparation helped him as he pursued cycling on the world stage. During the 1980s and '90s, his competitive career led him to a spot on the 1984 Olympic Team for his home country and, later, a bronze medal in the 1990 Commonwealth Games. All of this prepared him well for his next big opportunity.[21]

In 2003, Brailsford became the performance director for the British cycling team. He was embarking on a challenge that would define his career and secure his legacy.

The problem Brailsford was asked to solve was simple—the British team was irrelevant in the sport. They had not won an Olympic medal in seventy-six years, and no one from Britain had ever won the Tour de France. Brailsford's next steps were a clinic on Reinventing Continuously. He focused on progression, not perfection, and compounded the gains, a concept often referred to as marginal gains. Here's how it works.

Rather than fixate on the outcome, you drill down on the process. Of course, the desired outcome is still the goal, but a preoccupation with the desired outcome without action is ridiculous. Once again, hope is not a strategy. Once the outcome is clear, you go back upstream and identify all the individual and even miniscule steps in the process that you could improve. What could happen if you could become 1 percent better on the execution of many different inputs?

The concept of marginal gains is known by different names in different settings and parts of the world. The Japanese have a word for it—they call it Kaizen. This concept was made famous by the Toyota Production System and is discussed at length by consultants and authors worldwide. Beginning in 1951, Toyota began soliciting ideas for improvement from employees. Today, millions of individual ideas are submitted annually. Virtually no idea is too small; something as simple as moving a switch an arm's length away, to a button on the floor to reduce unnecessary motion and save time, will be adopted if the change will save a single second on the assembly line. This incremental improvement, compounded over time, will make a difference. This is marginal gains in action.[22]

Alan Weiss, consultant and PhD, boils it down simply: "If you improve by 1% a day, in 70 days you're twice as good." In practice, that looks like the following:[23]

- In three months, you will be 2.4 times better than today.
- In six months, you will be 6 times better than today.
- In twelve months, you will be 36 times better than you are today.

This simple focus on improving small, potentially even unnoticeable, portions of your work can compound and create significant impact over time. However, on the opposite side, James Clear, in *Atomic Habits,* reminds us, "If you get one percent worse each day for one year, you'll decline nearly down to zero."[24]

Back to Dave's story. What areas would he address to help his cycling team ascend the winner's podium? The improvements covered a wide spectrum of ideas from the expected to the novel. One such improvement was that the team made the strategic decision not to shake hands at the Olympics to avoid illness. We can also take note of a few of the other ideas that collectively created real, tangible benefits for the team.

Brailsford and his coaches began by making many small

adjustments—just the sort of things you would expect from a professional cycling team. They reengineered the bike seats for more comfort and treated the tires for better grip. They asked riders to wear special heated shorts to maintain ideal muscle temperature while riding, and they also began to use biofeedback sensors to monitor each athlete's performance during practice sessions.[25]

But they didn't stop there. Here is how Brailsford described some of their efforts in a *Harvard Business Review* article:

> By experimenting in a wind tunnel, we searched for small improvements to aerodynamics. By analyzing the mechanics area in the team truck, we discovered that dust was accumulating on the floor, undermining bike maintenance. So we painted the floor white, in order to spot any impurities. We hired a surgeon to teach our athletes about proper handwashing so as to avoid illnesses during competition. We were precise about food preparation. We brought our own mattresses and pillows so our athletes could sleep in the same posture every night. We searched for small improvements everywhere and found countless opportunities. Taken together, we felt they gave us a competitive advantage.[26]

For those of you who do not follow cycling, you may be wondering, *Did it work?* In a word, yes! Here are some of the results the team enjoyed under Dave's leadership.

In 2008 at the Beijing Olympics, his team won seven of ten gold medals. The team repeated the same feat four years later at the London Games. Brailsford is now coaching in the professional ranks. His team won the Tour de France in seven of eight years between 2012 and 2019. Along the way, Dave was knighted by the queen—he is now Sir Dave Brailsford.[27]

Reinventing anything is real work. Sometimes the new and improved approach may be simple in concept, but often, the implementation will be challenging. Stay the course! Every little bit of improvement matters!

Try This: If you could reinvent one thing in any of the three domains (self, systems, or structure), what would you choose and why? Who could help you? Why not start today?

For access to the FREE Uncommon Greatness digital self-assessment and help with your next steps, text **uncommon** to 66866 or scan the QR code in the Resources section at the end of the book.

REINVENT CONTINUOUSLY: IDEAS FOR ACTION

I f vision is the fire motivating a leader and an organization to move into an unknown future with confidence, the wood for the fire is found in this third Fundamental: Reinvent Continuously. For the best leaders, Reinvent Continuously is a practice, a mindset, and a personal discipline.

Following are three strategies for you to consider to help you increase your proficiency on this fun and high-impact Fundamental: **Think Different**, **Cultivate Creativity**, and **Lead Change**.

THINK DIFFERENT

What's your favorite ad campaign? You may have to think about that for a minute. For me, the answer is the *Think Different* campaign launched by Apple in 1997. Here are a few lines from the iconic television ad:[1]

Here's to the crazy ones. The misfits. The rebels. The troublemakers. The round pegs in square holes. The ones who see things differently . . . While some see them as the crazy ones, we see genius. Because the people who are crazy enough to think they can change the world are the ones who do.

How do you think differently, particularly if this is not your natural bent or bias? I have some ideas for your consideration.

Invest the Time. Where do ideas come from? For me, this question is impossible to answer. Their source is not the product of a replicable process. The great ideas can come in a eureka moment or as the result of years of inquiry, experimentation, and setbacks. However, there are inputs that can facilitate break-through ideas. Of all the elements I am aware of, the most precious and most often overlooked is time. I just admitted that sometimes a great idea is revealed in a moment of inspiration. However, this is both rare and often misinterpreted. In many of the flashes of inspiration, the problem had been simmering for weeks, months, or even years. Here's the truth about mining for great ideas—it typically takes time.

One egregious infraction I have seen repeated over and over throughout my career is the failure to invest adequate time when brainstorming.

In his book *What a Great Idea*, Chic Thompson cites research that reveals two levels of brainstorming. In Level One, the participants basically capture what is already known or has been tried previously. Depending on who is in the room, this phase typically requires forty-five minutes to complete. Only then can you move into Level Two. This is the domain of the new, novel, and unexpected.[2]

How many times in your life have you participated in a "failed" brainstorming session that was less than forty-five minutes? If you are not willing to invest the time, you'll never find the gold.

If you choose to use a technique like brainstorming with your team, increase the amount of time you are willing to invest; I suggest a minimum of ninety minutes. There's much more to say about this subject. If you want my Ten Tips for Brilliant Brainstorming, go to LeadEveryDay.com/uncommon.

Consider the Opposite. Several years ago, I was trying to help a nonprofit organization increase participation in their events. The team was bright, engaged, and eager to improve. At least they were fully engaged until I told them what we were going to do. Here's a condensed version of the conversation as I set up the day.

"Today, I know you want to think creatively about how to increase attendance at your events. I agree that would be a wonderful outcome. However, I want to ask a different question: *What would you need to do to depress attendance?*" They looked at me as if I had lost my mind. Remember, I was a guest facilitator. I'm assuming several members of the team thought to themselves, *Who invited this wacko?*

I could sense the tension in the room, but I pushed on. "I know this feels strange—let's just try this. I think it could be fun." Slowly and reluctantly, they began to share ideas ranging from the bizarre to the pedestrian.

"We could physically change the location of the event every

week and make folks find us. We could make it impossible to park. What if we were not friendly when people arrived? What if we took down all the wayfinding signage? We could constantly change the published event time—then, totally disregard it. Some weeks we could start late and other weeks we could blow past our stated end time."

I was capturing them all on flip chart pages and putting them on the wall. At several points the energy dropped and the ideas slowed to a crawl, but we persisted. We probably did this for two hours. At that point we had maybe 150 ideas.

I stopped the ideation and said, "Take a look at the list; do you see anything we should talk about?" The room sat in silence—it felt like an eternity while everyone read the list. Finally, one person raised their hand as if they needed my permission to share their observation.

"Uh . . . we do a lot of those things," he said sheepishly. I read the room and several were nodding in agreement. "Okay," I said. "Let's identify all the things on this list you currently do; we'll rank them based on their potential impact, and then we can start with the biggest opportunity and begin creating our action plan. You need to eradicate those behaviors and, in theory, your actions should increase participation."

There were obviously a number of paths we could have taken to identify ideas to improve event attendance—in this case, by choosing to consider the opposite, the team's next steps were obvious.

Ask More Questions. Questions are one of the most powerful tools at a leader's disposal. They are free, available in ample supply, can be used in most any situation, and, wielded wisely, can unlock a world of previously unknown options and opportunities.

There is so much to say here. I devoted an entire chapter in *Smart Leadership*, titled "Ask Don't Tell," to this topic. (If you want a free copy of that chapter, go to LeadEveryDay.com/uncommon.) For our purposes here, I want to challenge and encourage you: ask more and better questions.

When you ask a question, there are several potential benefits: You may learn something. You demonstrate your humility and vulnerability. You can also accelerate your learning when you ask a question that requires a synthesis or summary of a larger body of information.

One word about better questions. They come in all shapes and sizes. Here's one tip. Ask more open-ended questions. These are questions that require more than a one-word response. Did you enjoy the show? Closed-ended. The better question would be open-ended: What did you enjoy most about the show?

You may also want to monitor the number of questions you ask in a typical day. I'm not suggesting you actually count them; that could be weird. However, work to increase your awareness and identify your tendencies. With your newfound awareness, experiment with asking more questions. See what happens.

CULTIVATE CREATIVITY

Creativity is a must for great leadership. Unfortunately, I rarely hear the topic discussed in leadership circles. In part this is because of the different forms creativity takes in our world. The typical connotation is with artistic creativity. Artists are truly gifted individuals—they paint, draw, sculpt, and express things in beautiful and meaningful ways. When I hear leaders say they're not creative, they are thinking about artistic creativity. However, I am an ambassador for a different kind of creativity. The ability to *think* creatively.

Simply stated, creative thinking is the ability to generate viable options. When the skill of creative thinking is applied to our biggest problems and opportunities, a new world of possibilities emerges. Every leader on the planet needs to cultivate this form of creativity! Here are some tips for how to do so.

Expand Your World. Human beings cannot create from a vacuum. Our creative output is formed and informed by the experiences, knowledge, relationships, and skills we have amassed over our lifetimes. These are independent and cumulative variables. The richness of our creative output is a direct reflection of the breadth and depth of our inputs.

I often describe this part of the creative process as being like an artist commissioned to paint a masterpiece. The canvas represents the impact we'll have on the world. The artist's palette contains all the experiences, knowledge, relationships, and skills we have at our disposal—think of these as the paint. Let's take this one step further. You cannot use paint that is still in the tube. It must first be applied to the palette. Once there, you can blend the colors and use different brushes to create various effects on the canvas. The combinations are virtually endless if you have the colors to begin with. When we expand our world, we put more paint on the palette of our lives that can help us create our masterpiece. Here's my fear informed by my observations: far too many leaders have limited their creative potential because they have so few colors to work with.

There was a time early in my life when I was timid in this area. I don't know where this came from, but when confronted with new experiences or opportunities, I would draw back. Not anymore. When given the chance to put more paint on my canvas, I jump at the opportunity. Why the change? I realized that, someday, I might need the paint to complete my masterpiece.

Look at your calendar. What do you have on your calendar in the next thirty days that might help you expand your world? Is there a conversation, an event, a new restaurant, a trip to a new place that will add color to your palette? If not, try adding something.

Escape the Known. What is the greatest impediment to a better idea? The idea you are presently attached to. The best leaders can escape the known in order to explore other possibilities.

Dr. Edward de Bono is one of the world's preeminent thought leaders in the field of creative thinking. When I met Dr. de Bono, he was speaking at a TED conference. After his presentation, I approached him and asked if I could buy him a meal while he was in town. To my delight, he said yes. At that time, he had authored seventy-six books on creative thinking.[3]

One of the concepts he has written about is what he calls Blocked by Openness. He uses this example: If you have a regular route you travel to work, school, or wherever you are going, you are less likely to find a better route, even though one may exist. The absence of a barrier or obstacle is what keeps you from exploring, and perhaps discovering, a better way.

Most of the innovations in the world required someone to escape what was already known. When Galileo said the world was round, everyone *knew* it was flat. When the Wright brothers decided to turn their skills as bicycle mechanics into an aviation business, everyone *knew* heavier-than-air flying machines were a fantasy. In 1886, when Carl Benz decided to build the first commercially available automobile, people *knew* the horse and buggy was the way to travel.

These examples are world-changing for sure, but don't miss the principle. When you want to think creatively about anything, you will have to escape your own preconceived notions, and maybe the conventional wisdom of the world, and at least for a moment, put aside what you *know* to be true. If you do, you might just find a better way.

What are you sure of that might be blocking you from a better way? Consider your biggest current challenge. What are you sure is true? Set that aside, then consider how you would proceed if you couldn't continue with your current approach.

Train Your Brain. The brain is a self-optimizing memory system. This is generally a good thing and means our brains are hardwired for pattern recognition. This is a fantastic feature if you are a prehistoric person and encounter a predator. You don't want to try to figure out the friend or foe thing every time you see a lion. However, the little-discussed dark side of this feature, the bug if you will, is the brain's natural tendency to travel in well-worn paths. The patterns, by definition, require zero creativity. More than that, they are the barriers that block our creative instincts. These existing mental pathways become ruts.

Brain training, as it relates to creative thinking, can help you escape these ruts. In essence, you can develop the on-demand skill to jump out of the rut and pursue other mental pathways and the alternatives they hold. The best news is that there are scores of techniques to help you do this. These range from brainstorming to streaming, or jamming as it is sometimes called, to quota system—a simple idea of setting a predetermined quota for the number of ideas you will create before you make your final decision on the way forward. Other techniques include reversal, mind mapping, and, one of my personal favorites, random input. This is not a book on the techniques to stimulate creative thinking. However, it is a skill within your reach. It's not as hard as running a marathon or learning a foreign language. However, the principles are the same. You must commit and then train. When you do, you'll be amazed at what your mind can accomplish.

Buy a book containing techniques to spur your creative thinking. There are many out there with new ones always in the works. Commit to try a new technique every few weeks. If you take this challenge, remember two things.

One, you will most likely have an affinity for some of the approaches and, with others, not so much. Be careful: being uncomfortable with something doesn't mean you can't learn to master it. Remember the first time you, or your child, tried to ride a bike?

Two, you will also discover that some techniques are better suited to one situation than another. For example, brainstorming is a group activity requiring a significant time investment while streaming (also known as jamming or brain-writing) is a solo activity requiring just a few minutes. Think of the various techniques like tools; sometimes you need a hammer and other times the task at hand requires a screwdriver. Fill your toolbox for the unexpected opportunities in your future!

LEAD CHANGE

The nature of change has changed. Change in the modern organization is nonlinear, interdependent, iterative, and never-ending . . . and the number of changes being implemented at any given time can be overwhelming. This new normal has created a blizzard, often with whiteout conditions for leaders and frontline associates. How does the leader respond? It depends.

Different types of changes require different interventions. There is no longer a linear process for leading change. Successful change requires more of a systems-thinking approach. Leaders must stay grounded in the realities of their organizations and the change initiatives they launch more than ever before. They must judge the readiness of their organization for the next change. They must discern the impact of recent changes. Leaders must consider the historical context. You must decide when to iterate and when to stay the course. You must determine how much support is needed for a particular change and what form that support should take. You need to be attuned to the spirit of the people—when do they need to hear the vision again? Do they need to hear it differently? You must gauge the energy of the organization and deputize others to help keep the change flames burning.

Change is not a burden to be carried by the leader; it should not be viewed as a distraction or something to be endured. To create and sustain productive and purposeful change is the ultimate responsibility of every leader. We must become masters of the art of organizational change. Following are some key actions leaders can take to make change a reality.

Maintain Dynamic Awareness. To respond well to this

onslaught of competing inputs, leaders must maintain deep knowledge regarding what is happening in their organization at all times. Dynamic Awareness requires the leader to constantly shift their focus to determine where to invest their energy and resources. Done well, Dynamic Awareness is proactive, empathetic, continuous, and immersive. Dynamic Awareness is essential for every leader, but it becomes critical when in service of a desired change.

There are three questions that can help you strengthen your Dynamic Awareness when applied to your change efforts.

1. What's happening?
2. What does it mean?
3. What should we do about it?

Dynamic Awareness (and these questions) should be applied to four essential elements required for successful change: communication, leadership, support, and experimentation. Being Dynamically Aware will tell you which of these components you must focus on at any given point in time to drive the change forward! Without Dynamic Awareness, successful and sustainable change will always remain just out of your reach.

Communicate Tirelessly. Our team has been researching the topic of organizational change for the last few years, and our formal work will not be completed for another year or more. So, I'm not sure exactly what will make the final list or the language we may ultimately publish. However, I am confident based on what we have already learned that communication is a key driver of successful change efforts.

As you can imagine, communication in the context of change

takes many forms. There are at least three required types: vision, encouragement, and progress.

The vision needs to portray a preferred future. The destination should have benefit for the organization and, by extension, the people. Whenever possible, these future benefits should energize people. Next, the vision needs to be dynamic as opposed to rigid. The bigger the change effort, the less likely the vision will manifest itself exactly as it was originally cast. The leaders need a spirit of flexibility as they describe a developing picture of the future.

Change is typically hard. Combine this with the fact that the burden of implementing the desired change in many cases falls on the frontline employees, and you have a perfect opportunity to lift the spirit of people with your encouragement. The leader's words carry a lot of weight—use them wisely.

If you cast a compelling picture of the future and people choose to follow you, they will expect progress reports. You have a perspective many in the organization do not. You can see across your industry and across departments; you have forecasts and projections that the majority do not see. Regular progress updates will bring energy to your change efforts.

There's at least one more factor for consideration as it relates to communication during a change effort: strategic repetition.

Chick-fil-A employees are known across the country for their hospitality. One signature phrase that encapsulates the spirit of the culture is "my pleasure." How did this become the norm in three thousand independently operated restaurants? In part, strategic repetition.

Every year for a *decade*, when Chick-fil-A's founder, Truett Cathy, addressed leadership at our annual meeting, he said,

"When someone says, 'Thank you,' what do we say? 'My plea-sure.'" The first couple of years, Mr. Cathy provided the response. In the years that followed, the audience knew the answer and would, in full voice, say, "My pleasure." During a change effort, strategic repetition is critical. What change have you been will-ing to champion personally for a decade?

Expand Leadership. Change efforts fail for many reasons. Two of the most common are that the change loses the energy required to see it through or that the organization lacks the patience to stay the course. You probably know this; many or-ganizations suffer from attention deficit hyperactivity disorder (ADHD). Leaders as a group are very easily distracted.

One strategy to combat both pitfalls is to Expand Leader-ship. Ultimately, for the change to become embedded in the or-ganization, you'll want everyone to buy in. But to get to this point, the first place to begin is among your leaders—preferably those in your inner circle. There are a few very pragmatic reasons to start with them.

If people have questions about the change, they will typically not come to you. They will go to another leader lower in the or-ganization. You don't want these leaders to say, "I don't know." You want them to be ambassadors for the change.

Given the sheer number of changes, you, as the point leader, cannot lead every change effort. You will need others to step up to this task. You may publicly deputize them or appoint them so everyone knows they have your support, but you can probably not "own" the day-to-day issues associated with every change.

Finally, it will be much easier to sustain the energy needed if you have delegated and empowered another leader to cham-pion a specific change. You also inject additional energy into the process if you ask for periodic reports on progress. Change requires energy; leaders are the source of that energy.

Provide Support. Every change effort requires support. This is a big topic with many different elements. What determines the types of support? The nature of the change and the needs of the people. Here are some examples: training, resources, tools, technology, information, coaching, metrics, ongoing communications, and more. By the way, what is required during a change effort can change over time. You may think you have it figured out before you even launch the project. Then, once the change hits the street, you realize adjustments are necessary. You may discover that something entirely different than anything you imagined is exactly what the people need to move the change forward. This is one more example where the Dynamic Awareness of leaders is required for long-term, sustained success.

Identify a major, or even a more modest, change initiative currently underway in your organization. Go to people from three different levels who are actively involved in implementation of the desired change. (Be sure to include someone from the front lines.) Ask them one question: What additional support do you need to make this change effort more successful?

Experiment Often. Over the years, I've had the privilege to spend some time with folks from the Stanford Design School (the d.school). Some of their professors have served on several of our research teams over the last decade. One of the things I love about the philosophy they teach at the d.school is the concept of test and learn. A willingness to experiment is essential for successful change.

The larger the change, the more loosely you should hold the

methods and the plan. Things change, the world shifts, and you need to adapt. If you fail to iterate often, you will probably fail.

The caution here is to not fall prey to the ADHD I referenced earlier. Some ideas take time to implement and even longer to embed. In the beginning, nothing is easy, and success may be hard to discern. Yet again, this is why the leader needs Dynamic Awareness. When is it time to tweak the plan or change the process? When should the team be challenged to stay the course? These are important moments in which judgment is required. Even if the answer is stay the course . . . for now, this does not mean that future iteration is off the table. The best leaders always reserve the right to get smarter. They listen, learn, observe, and repeat the process over and over again.

Look around your organization in search of a change project that is floundering, maybe even stuck. Talk to the people leading this specific change project. Ask them three questions:

- If you could do it all again, what would you do differently?
- Which of those insights could you apply now to restart, redirect, or reenergize this work?
- What additional support do you need to move this work forward?

What's your favorite part of leadership? As we've already established, all the Fundamentals must be present at a baseline competency level in order to lead well. But I'm guessing you'll have one of the Fundamentals you enjoy the most. For me, to Reinvent Continuously is the most fun and probably the most rewarding.

Without reinvention, our vision will not be achievable. As mentioned earlier, your current systems, work processes, and behaviors are perfectly aligned to the outcomes you are achieving. Chances are high they were not designed to support or move you toward your future vision. The challenge you and your team face can be summarized in a simple question: *What needs to change in order to make progress toward our vision?* Nothing improves without change.

If you are thoughtful, strategic, and diligent regarding your reinvention efforts, the people you serve and the organization that employs you will ultimately thank you.

Don't fear change . . . create it. Reinvention is the fuel of progress.

REINVENT CONTINUOUSLY
BEST PRACTICES AND KEY STRATEGIES

Think Different
- Invest the Time
- Consider the Opposite
- Ask More Questions

Cultivate Creativity
- Expand Your World
- Escape the Known
- Train Your Brain

Lead Change
- Maintain Dynamic Awareness
- Communicate Tirelessly
- Expand Leadership
- Provide Support
- Experiment Often

Fundamental #4

VALUE RESULTS AND RELATIONSHIPS

RELEASE THE POWER

*The genius of the **and** is about embracing complexity
and finding ways to navigate it with creativity and ingenuity.*

JIM COLLINS

The Rocket Chemical Company and its three employees had a dream to serve the emerging aerospace community. Founded in 1953, they set out to create a water-displacing product that would be used to prevent corrosion on critical parts of the Atlas rocket. Their first thirty-nine attempts failed. On their fortieth try, they landed on the formula for what the world now knows as WD-40. The Rocket Chemical Company officially changed their name to WD-40 in 1969.[1] During the early years, the company maintained steady growth with a surge of 61 percent in share value the day they joined the NASDAQ in 1993.[2]

For those of you who are not familiar with WD-40, the company's website says it protects metal from rust and corrosion, penetrates stuck parts, displaces moisture, and lubricates almost anything. It even removes grease, grime, and more from most surfaces. Their site goes on to share two-thousand-plus uses for the product as submitted by their customers.

Garry Ridge joined the company in 1987 and ten years later became the company's CEO. Even with a background in the oil and gas industry and a decade of experience in the company, Ridge says he was still scared about his new role. So he decided to go back to school and see what he could learn that would help him be a better CEO. He enrolled in the Masters of Executive Leadership program at San Diego State University, where he met Ken Blanchard.[3]

In one of the classes taught by Blanchard, Ridge heard the story from early in Ken's career of how he was always in trouble because of one specific, and some thought peculiar, practice. On the first day of each course, he would give the students a copy of the final exam. The other faculty and administration objected. Blanchard's response: "Not only am I going to give them the final exam questions on the first day . . . I'm going to spend the rest of the semester teaching them the answers. I want everyone to get an 'A'!"[4]

Ridge was intrigued by this idea. What would happen if he could help everyone in his organization get an A? His strategy going forward would be to help his leaders Value Results *and* Relationships. This was a defining moment for Ridge and WD-40. They completely revamped their performance management system so that there would be three parts:

- Performance planning—the employee and supervisor agree on what an A would look like.

- Ongoing coaching, including ninety-day check-ins to help everyone get their A.
- A year-end review where everyone receives their grade.[5]

Does this approach work? Ridge and his tribe, the term WD-40 uses to describe their people, would say yes! Let's start with the financials.

During his tenure as CEO, market capitalization has risen from $275 million to more than $2.5 billion. This growth has been powered by the brand's global expansion—today, WD-40 is sold in 176 countries and, according to one survey from a few years ago, the company reports their product can be found in 80 percent of American homes.[6, 7]

These numbers are impressive, but what's really behind them? Ridge would tell you their success has been largely driven by seriously attempting to help every employee get an A. Here's how the employees evaluated their experience working for the company:[8]

"I am clear on the company's goals"—**97.2 percent**.

"I am excited about WD-40 Company's future direction"—**93.4 percent**.

"WD-40 Company encourages employees to continually improve in their job"—**92.9 percent**.

"I understand how my job contributes to achieving WD-40 Company's goals"—**97.9 percent**.

"I know what results are expected of me"—**97.4 percent**.

"I feel my opinions and values are a good fit with the WD-40 Company culture"—**98.1 percent**.

"I love to tell people that I work for WD-40 Company"—**99.0 percent**.

VALUE RESULTS AND RELATIONSHIPS

What Garry Ridge did was extraordinary. From what I have been able to learn about him, he made this Fundamental look easy. For most of us, it will not be easy.

I believe to consistently Value Results *and* Relationships will be the most challenging of the Fundamentals for the majority of leaders. The rationale behind this statement is simple: almost every leader I've ever met is either more results-oriented *or* more relationship-oriented.

This a not a problem *if* the leader acknowledges their bias and compensates accordingly. This is eminently doable, but before we get to the how, I want to invest a little time explaining what it means to Value Results and Relationships.

When I find myself in a one-on-one conversation, I have a reputation for drawing on napkins. If you and I were having a cup of coffee and discussing this topic, that is exactly what I would do. I would sketch out something that looks like this:

Results ●————————————● Relationships

Then I would hand you the pen and ask you to put an X where you typically land on this continuum. Next, I would ask you where you think you should be. This is a bit of a trick question—heck, this Fundamental is Value Results *and* Relationships, so most people would assume the correct answer would be in the center. That is not the goal. Then, as a leader, you would have little passion for results *or* relationships! I suggest an alternative answer.

You want to escape the trap I set for you, and the one we often set for ourselves. Don't choose mediocrity. Escape the continuum and Value *both* Results and Relationships.

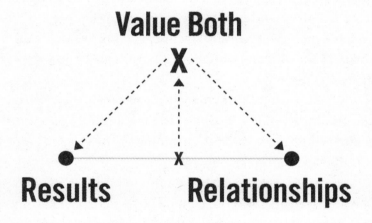

Jim Collins has had a profound impact on my thinking over the years as, surely, he has on many of you as well. I have had the opportunity to spend some time with him in Boulder, and he has spoken for our organization on a couple of occasions. This Fundamental is a fabulous example of something Jim teaches. While researching his book *Built to Last*, Jim's team discovered the most successful companies demonstrate a principle he calls the "genius of the and."

Value Results *and* Relationships is a perfect example of Jim's discovery. Organizations and leaders who can embrace the tension between two, sometimes opposing, conditions, values, beliefs, or expectations enjoy a disproportionate return. There is certainly a tension when conflicting objectives are present. However, the tension creates friction, energy, creativity, and progress. If you can harness that energy, you will reap the benefits.[9]

For many leaders, this is a difficult concept. For some, it is a hill they cannot climb. Not that it is too high or treacherous. The route is known and guides are prevalent. What prevents many leaders from new levels of influence and effectiveness is their inability or unwillingness to accept the truth about how they show up as a leader.

What are people thinking when you enter a room? What are you thinking? Your willingness to own and mitigate your bias could well be the greatest determining factor in your influence, contribution, career, and legacy.

I assume I could say this about any of the Fundamentals, but now feels like the right moment to share something with you. If you don't *want to* develop this Fundamental, you will never do it. You will not wake up one morning miraculously freed from your previous bias and mindset. You must want to Value *both* Results *and* Relationships—and then, do the work to make it so.

Assuming you've made the decision to do this, the next step to harness the power of this Fundamental is to own your bias. Regardless of where you are today, it's okay. The next chapter will provide ample ideas for action, but regarding this first step, if you don't know your bias, ask anyone who lives with you or works with you; they will know.

A quick word for those of you who possess a natural bias for both results and relationships: the joke I've been using for decades—I don't like you!

If this is you, congratulations! You won't have to work on this Fundamental as the other 95 percent of the leaders in the world and I do. Please don't be smug. Be thankful.

Like most things in life, accomplishment is the product of disciplined action and practice over time. You may struggle with this for a season, or perhaps forever, but along the way, you may experience a moment of clarity. For me, it was a conversation with our former company president. Just a little context will be helpful.

Earlier in my career, I was asked to move to our Field Operations department and lead a significant portion of the team that served our local Operators. I was actually told by the president that I had been selected because of my results orientation. Keep in mind, this was before we formally established our organization's Fundamentals of Leadership. When he gave me the job, he did offer a cautionary note: "As you raise the value of results, be sure you do not lower the value we place on relationships. You must keep the value high on both." I understood my marching orders, or so I thought.

A few months into the role, our team decided we needed to terminate the relationship we had with one of our restaurant Operators. Now, I'll put that in perspective—our retention rate at the time was hovering around 96 percent and had been at that level for decades. Terminating an agreement was such a big deal,

I had to go present the case to the president. If he agreed with my recommendation, he would take it to our founder. This was my first recommendation of this type.

I presented my case. He listened patiently and said, "I agree . . . not now." I was confused. I didn't know what to say next, so I repeated my recommendation and offered a quick re-cap of our thought process. He said, "I heard you the first time and I agree with your recommendation . . . just not now." At this point I voiced my confusion. Here's what he said.

"I agree with your conclusion and the rationale you and the team used to reach your recommendation. However, it is a week before Thanksgiving. This leader has done nothing unethical or illegal. Therefore, we are not going to send him home to his family this week to tell them he lost his business. You can have the conversation with him in January."

I was speechless. I walked away from that meeting with a lot more than a decision about this single situation. I gained a glimpse of what it means to Value Results *and* Relationships.

I still struggle with this Fundamental, but I'll never forget that moment. The best leaders overcome their personal bias and learn to Value *both* Results and Relationships.

PEDAL TO THE METAL

Ross Brawn was introduced to motor racing at an early age by his father. His dad, an engineer, instilled a love for the sport in the boy. Ross's fascination would ultimately bloom into a passion that propelled him to become one of the most successful figures in the history of Formula 1 racing.

Brawn studied engineering at the University of Reading.

After initially being rejected for his dream job, he was called back for the role one year after he first submitted his application. The person who had been selected ahead of him had washed out. So, with what could be qualified as a slow start, the legendary career officially began on a shop floor as an apprentice to a machinist in 1976. This grounding in the craft of automaking would not only mark the young Brawn, but it would also help distinguish him. He was quickly recognized as a rare talent.

His first big break came in 1991, when Brawn became the technical director for the Benetton team. He helped the team win back-to-back world championships in 1994 and 1995.[10]

Team Ferrari had a rich history you could trace back to the roots of the sport, but they had fallen on hard times—they had not won a world championship in twenty years. They were convinced that Brawn could help. In 1996, Ferrari lured Brawn away from Benetton.

At Ferrari, Brawn found a team in shambles. I think he might even challenge the existence of a real team. The behaviors he described are much more descriptive of a work group, a group of people fulfilling their individual responsibilities but without the benefit of the collaboration or creativity of others. Without a shared sense of ownership for the whole, they are a team in name only.

In the case of Ferrari, these individuals appeared to be working really hard, but they were not working together. One example is the fact that the chassis for the cars and the engines were built in different countries. At his core, Brawn saw the car as a unified expression of an idea that could not be created as independent parts and merely bolted together. He understood instinctively, and from experience, that the people needed to work together to create the magic.

This belief fueled his passion to invest heavily in the relationships between him and the teams and the relationships among team members. He was masterful at building teams and valuing the individuals who could do the impossible over and over again, year after year. For Brawn, unity became a theme during the turnaround at Ferrari and throughout his career.[11]

One of his early moves was to relocate the engine department from England to Italy. For Brawn, this was much more than a symbolic move. He wanted these two teams to live, work, and play together. He wanted them to do life together—late-night trips to the local pub were part of Brawn's playbook.[12]

Another moment of clarity, perhaps a breakthrough, came when Brawn was on the shop floor and asked a mechanic to point him to the washroom. The mechanic said, "Yours is upstairs," pointing to the executive offices. Brawn reframed his question: "Where is the closest washroom?" The mechanic pointed to the one on the shop floor. Brawn excused himself and visited that facility. The ripple effect of this simple action is hard to overstate. Word spread like wildfire—"The boss used our washroom!"[13]

Who knows? If Brawn had not grown up on the shop floor, would he have made the same decision? Maybe. However, with this simple action, and likely many other similarly symbolic gestures, he established the credibility that every leader needs. He was showing them what "one team" and unity looked like. It worked. During his run at Ferrari, Brawn's focus on the results and relationships led the team to win five world championships in five years.

After leaving Ferrari in 2006, Brawn took a break and then joined Honda in 2008, but shortly thereafter the company decided to exit the sport. Brawn and others banded together to purchase the team. Their new team, called Brawn GP, won a championship in 2008—their first season in competition. A few years later, Brawn sold the team to Mercedes and stayed on as the team principal. During his time with Mercedes, they won multiple championships.[14]

What made Brawn such an icon in F1 racing? The number of championships is a good place to start—his teams won sixteen during his career. However, how he did it is instructive for leaders everywhere. His illustrious career was always fueled by a relentless pursuit of results while he never lost sight of the importance of the people who could bring his lofty aspirations to fruition. Brawn believed passionately that he needed to Value Results and Relationships.

THEY CALL ME COACH

As you look back over your career, are there days that stand out for you? I assume the answer is yes. The day you crushed your first big presentation to the board. Maybe the day you were hired, or a memorable day when you received a well-earned promotion. I trust you have a lot of those in your memory banks. One of mine was an afternoon a colleague of mine and I spent with the legendary coach John Wooden.

Coach was ninety-five years old at the time. He ultimately spoke to our organization after he turned ninety-six. During our visit, he was warm, sharp, curious, and fully engaged. What a treat to spend time with him in his home. He lived in a small condominium in Westwood, Los Angeles, that he and his wife, Nell, had purchased many decades before. During our conversation he mentioned Bill had not called yet, but he expected him to before the day was over. Because I had done my homework, I knew exactly who he was referring to.

Bill Walton, the National Basketball Association Hall of Famer and two-time Naismith Award winner, played for Coach Wooden at UCLA from 1970 to 1974. During his tenure, the team won two national championships.[15]

Why would the coach be expecting a call from Bill? Because Bill called almost every day and had been doing so for nearly forty years. Wait, a player called his coach every day for decades—what's up with that? The coach told us that many of his former players called often. I think it's because Coach Wooden Valued Results and Relationships.

There are many stories of the coach's exceptional attention to the details of the game. He is famously known for using time in the first practice of the year to teach players how to put on their socks correctly. He told them if they did not, they would get blisters that would hinder their play, and if they didn't play well, he would lose his job.[16]

The offseason was the perfect opportunity to improve the team's execution, which the coach believed was a direct reflection of his performance. Wooden would take some facet of the game and focus intently on it the entire offseason—one year it was dribbling, another year it was rebounding. He would watch the game footage of the best players, interview them if he could, call their coaches, read what had been written on the topic, and then change his practice drills and disciplines to incorporate his insights. This and many other examples point to the fact the coach valued results.

On the relationship front, he was known to care deeply about his players. This was demonstrated in many ways over the years with individual situations. He knew their interests off the court, their hobbies, and their hopes and dreams. The coach loved his players. He attended weddings and visited his players in the hospital well beyond his days at UCLA.

Reflecting on his time with the coach, Gail Goodrich said, "He loved people, and had this tremendous gift to communicate with everyone, regardless of age or background. He always considered himself a teacher, and a teacher he was. When I played for him, he taught me the game of basketball. Later I came to realize, he really taught me the valuable aspects of life."

Coach wanted all his players to be successful on the court and in life. He documented his approach in what he called his Pyramid of Success. Coach gave me a framed and signed copy after our visit.

The pyramid contains fifteen character traits, fourteen of them undergirding the pinnacle—Competitive Greatness. Supporting traits include team spirit, friendship, and cooperation.[17]

The coach valued relationships so much so that, beyond being their coach, for many of his players, he became much more—a mentor, counselor, and friend. That's why decades after they left the locker room together for the last time, the coach was expecting a call from Bill. The two continued this daily ritual until the coach passed away in 2010. Who on your team is going to be calling you in thirty years? Why would they?

Try This: Do they think you are more results-oriented or relationship-oriented? If you have any doubt regarding your results versus relationship bias, ask three people who know you well to name it for you. When they share their perspective, don't argue, debate, deflect, deny, or rationalize their input. The only two things you can say are, "Please tell me more" and "Thank you." Owning your bias is the first step to Valuing both Results and Relationships.

For access to the FREE Uncommon Greatness digital self-assessment and help with your next steps, text **uncommon** to 66866 or scan the QR code in the Resources section at the end of the book.

VALUE RESULTS AND RELATIONSHIPS: IDEAS FOR ACTION

Leadership has its share of apparent contradictions: short-term profitability versus long-term investments to ensure a vibrant future; what the customers want versus what makes sense operationally; the need to protect our past while creating a different, preferred future; and others. Perhaps none of these tensions is as real or as important as the need to Value Results and Relationships. In this chapter, we'll go deep on three strategies to help you navigate this challenging Fundamental: **Set the Example**, **Coach for Success**, and **Demonstrate Care**.

SET THE EXAMPLE

I promise this is the last time I'll say this: people always watch the leader. They are trying to determine the answer to at least three questions: What's important? Are you trustworthy? Do you care about me? The order of these may differ depending on the individual, but all three of these questions are always in play.

Regarding the first question, "What's important?," your example is what people will look to first to find the answer they seek. The following tactics will help you steward your influence well.

Know the Values. What are your organization's core values? Your organization may or may not have stated values. What are the values for your team, department, or division? Perhaps you are not a fan of "values." Some leaders are not. If you fall in that category, let me reframe the question—I'll give you a few options.

- What commitments are you expecting your team to make to you and the organization?
- How do you want people to work in your organization?
- What are the behavioral norms you want to see demonstrated as people do their jobs?

Pick any of these questions you like and figure out the answer. You must know the answer to the question before you can create the context for consistent execution. I use the term *consistent* intentionally here. If you select good people (and who doesn't try to do that?), you will see flashes of brilliance. However, if you decide personal excellence is your answer to one of the questions above, and if modeled and activated over time, you will see more than flashes—you will begin to see patterns, and then at some point personal excellence will be the standard. This quest begins with you knowing your values.

Share the Values. If you know your values, you are ahead of the game. A lot of leaders have not yet articulated the beliefs they want to drive the behavior of their team, department, or organization. Next, you must begin the never-ending journey to Share the Values. As you share your values, people will begin to see your heart, passion, example, and leadership.

Tell stories of fellow employees who are bringing the values to life in their own way. Look for every opportunity to personalize the values with stories from your own life and leadership. What do the values mean to you? Do others know?

Constantly look for fresh ways to illustrate and illuminate the values. A team at Oracle went as far as to gamify their values, offering points to employees who demonstrated the values in their work. This created a positive feedback loop of recognition and reinforced the values to employees.[1] If you can keep them fresh in your heart and mind, they can remain relevant to your team. If they become stale to you, it will show in your words and actions.

Look at your calendar for the next thirty days. Identify at least a dozen specific opportunities to share one or more of your values. This could include one-on-one meetings, team meetings, new employee orientation, conversations with vendors, interviews with potential employees, encounters with your customers, an upcoming sales pitch, and more! Make it your mission to become the chief ambassador of your values.

Compensate for Your Bias. To set the example on this Fundamental will be challenging for most of you—it is for me! This does not mean you cannot excel at Valuing Results and Relationships; it does mean you probably have some work to do. The process to improve in this area is straightforward. Own your bias and put mechanisms in place to strengthen that which you don't do naturally well.

If you don't know whether you possess a results or a relationships bias, just ask anyone who knows you well. They know. (You may have already noted this suggestion from the Try This suggestion at the end of the previous chapter.) If the people you ask are unsure, or you get mixed responses, you may be part of a very small group of leaders who value both with little or no effort. If this is you, congratulations. Your leadership journey will be easier than most. However, if you do have a bias, you must compensate. Regardless of what you learn, you now know the truth about your bias—own it.

Next, you need to put mechanisms in place to help strengthen either your results orientation or your relationship orientation. There are countless tactics you can employ to compensate for your bias. Here are a few of them: Who are the people who see the world differently than you do? Specifically, who has a different bias than yours regarding results and relationships? Be sure to keep those people close and listen intently to their perspective.

What practices can you employ to offset your natural tendency? If you are more results-oriented, purposely engage in some relationship-oriented activities like one-on-one time with people or writing notes of appreciation. You can also include these in your personal plan if you want to track your progress. For those of you with a relationship bias, consider setting and sharing some tangible goals or schedule performance conversations with all of your direct reports on a regular basis.

COACH FOR SUCCESS

What do you believe about people and performance? I have chosen to believe that everyone wants to be successful. The trick for us as leaders is to help them. Truett Cathy, the founder of Chick-fil-A, challenged me decades ago to build my career on helping people be successful. What great advice for any leader!

Before we move on, let me address an idea that may be lurking in your mind: *It's not my job to help people be successful.* Well, we could debate the finer points of your perspective, but let me move to the bottom line. My response is simply this: Why not? Why not embrace the opportunity to unearth and ignite human potential? If you can, everyone wins. Now, if the person decides they do not want to do what is required, or you determine that they cannot do what is expected, I think you are off the hook. Between today and the point at which you reach this determination, you have a tremendous opportunity to Coach for Success.

Embrace the Role. If you were going to describe the way you approach your role as a leader, would you include coaching as part of your job? More and more, we live in a do-it-yourself (DIY) world. You can google how to change the oil in your car or install a sink. I fear many organizations have forced their leaders to adopt a DIY mindset when it comes to their own development. Unfortunately, to coach yourself well is nearly impossible. Here are a few reasons the people you lead need your coaching.

You can see things they cannot. I've had many coaches in my life—best I can estimate, over a hundred of them. I grew up playing numerous sports—baseball, football, tennis, basketball, and, as an adult, I started playing golf. I've also had a life coach and public speaking coaches.

One of the greatest gifts a coach can provide is perspective. Specifically, when you're working on form or technique, a coach can see things you physically cannot see—you are too close to or are engaged in the process of doing the thing. Where is my elbow on my backswing? I don't know. I can't see it while I'm swinging the club, but the coach can. How is my posture when approaching a serve on the tennis court? I have no idea. When you assume the role of a coach, you will see things, helpful things, that the learner cannot see without your help.

You have knowledge, skills, and experience they don't. Let's pretend I do see some things on my own. Perhaps I see that I am closing far fewer sales than others on my team. The identification of a problem is significant, but more important is how to resolve the issue. Because of their background and experience, a good coach can not only help you see the problem or opportunity, but they can also help you solve it. Some of the drills I have been given by coaches have been transformational in my life and leadership—not as much in my sporting endeavors but in my daily life.

Your opinion carries disproportionate weight. If a peer suggests something, that is one thing, but if your coach (supervisor/boss) suggests something, it matters more. You shouldn't gloss over this fact. This gives you a huge advantage when trying to help someone be successful. As long as they believe you really do want to help them win, your words will not only be weighty, but they'll also be welcomed.

Update your job description—not literally, but in your mind. Embrace the role of a coach. The next time you meet with a member of your team, imagine you are wearing a hat that says COACH on the front. See if this added role changes how you think about the conversation.

Provide Situational Coaching. Do you have a coaching style? Have you ever thought about it? Until I met Ken Blanchard, I hadn't given the topic much, or enough, thought. Honestly, my thinking on the topic was . . . lazy.

If you had asked me forty years ago what the best coaches do, I would probably have said something like, "They watch the team/individual/employee do their thing and then tell them how to improve." In retrospect, I was not paying attention. I now have full appreciation for how the best coaches embrace a much more nuanced and sophisticated approach to this skill set we call coaching.

My moment of clarity was when I was introduced to situational leadership, a concept pioneered by Ken Blanchard and Paul Hersey. The scope and implications of their work are too far-reaching to go into here. What I do want to do is raise your awareness on a topic I wish I had known much earlier in my career. Here's my summary of their insight.[2]

Every great leader/coach has multiple coaching styles at their disposal. Which one to use should *never* be determined by the leader's personal bias or preference. The style employed should always be determined by two factors—the task at hand and the competency level of the individual charged with the task.

You should match your coaching style with where the individual is on a competency curve. Tragically, too many leaders have a go-to style of coaching. This works smashingly well in only a fraction of situations. The rest of the time, our coaching is just not helpful or is insufficient. To be sure this is not feeling too abstract or academic, I'll share my interpretation and summary of Blanchard and Hersey's work.

If a person has no experience with a task, Ken calls them an enthusiastic beginner. The coaching style this person needs should be more **Directive**. For example, "Here's how to do XYZ."

If someone has experience but lacks critical skills, a more collaborative approach will be appropriate. Ken calls this a **Coaching** style. I think of this as a teaching style.

If someone has the experience and the skills but for whatever reason is lacking confidence or commitment, what they need is a more **Supportive** approach.

Finally, if someone has both the competence and the confidence, what they need from their coach/leader is effective **Delegation**. By the way, if you are a delegator by nature, be very careful. When you delegate to an enthusiastic beginner, they will struggle mightily or fail. For these individuals, see the first approach above: **Directive**.

Here's the point. Coaching others is not optional if you are committed to helping the people in your world be more successful. The next time you are faced with an opportunity to coach someone, stop and adjust your approach to meet them where they are.

Give Great Feedback. What does great feedback look like? Based on what you just read, we know it should be offered in the style appropriate to the competency and confidence of the person executing the task. True, but there are more attributes to make feedback most helpful.

Before I share a few ideas with you, think about the best feedback you ever received. Take a moment; this should be a pleasant memory. What makes feedback a gift? I challenge you to jot down a few ideas in the margin of this book. Now, let's look at my short list. How does my list compare with yours?

In order to provide great feedback, it must be honest, complete, timely, and actionable.

- Be Honest—If someone is going to give me feedback, I want them to tell me the truth. No one wins if someone tells you something was great when it was not.
- Empty the Tank—I have been challenged for years to share the "last 10 percent." I encourage you to do the same. In many situations we almost tell the whole truth

and then we draw back. The most value is always in the last 10 percent. If you're on the receiving end of feedback, you may want to just ask, "What's the last 10 percent?" You'll be glad you did.

- Respond Quickly—Feedback doesn't age well. If someone says, "Hey, I want to give you some feedback on something you said in a meeting a few months ago," I will certainly hear them out, but the value of their comments will be muted. I would conclude that conversation by saying, "Thank you! If anything like that comes up in the future, I would love the feedback at the end of the meeting."

- Make It Actionable—If you tell someone you didn't like their PowerPoint slides, that's not necessarily actionable. However, if you say something to the effect of, "I think it would be a good idea for you to use our colors and brand standards when creating your next presentation," that's actionable.

Praise Progress. Leaders love progress, and so do individual contributors. People love progress even more when it is acknowledged by their leader. I know a lot of leaders who have perfectionist tendencies; I can fall into that trap as well. I want my work to reflect personal excellence. As long as this is not taken too far, I'm not sure it is a totally bad thing. However, an unintended consequence of this bias can be a reluctance to praise the progress you see along the way.

Think about a time in your career when a leader praised the progress you and/or your team had made on an important body of work. Progress acknowledged does several things:

- Builds confidence
- Fuels engagement
- Gives hope
- Recognizes effort
- Reinforces the goal

Recognition has other benefits. According to a study by Bersin & Associates with 834 organizations, companies that scored in the top 20 percent for building a "recognition-rich culture" actually had 31 percent lower voluntary turnover rates.[3]

Don't become the leader no one wants to see coming. Don't be the leader who has a critical spirit. Be a leader who lifts the spirit of the people who are trying to accomplish the same goals you are. Praise Progress!

Over the next week, look for at least half a dozen opportunities to praise the progress an individual or the team has made on important work.

DEMONSTRATE CARE

This section includes several tactics to help you Demonstrate Care. Let me be clear: if you don't care deeply about the people you lead, no tactic you'll find in this book or any other will help you. If you are to Demonstrate Care for people, you must care about people. If this is a challenge for you, you may want to skip to the section titled "Embody a Leader's Heart."

One of the often-unrealized opportunities leaders face on a daily basis is to Demonstrate Care for those they lead. I am thankful to have worked my entire career in an organization that has always encouraged and modeled this behavior. Does your organization do the same? Regardless of your organization's posture on this issue, you can Demonstrate Care. The rewards for you as the leader, and the dividends for the organization, will be huge. The following tactics should prove helpful.

Practice Deep Listening. Several years ago, I found a beautiful and helpful metaphor to describe what I have been calling deep listening. Imagine a piece of sheet music; even if you aren't a musician, you know what one looks like—you have the staff, the notes themselves, and any number of other notations. To the untrained eye, you could easily assume these notes represent the music. You would be wrong. The notes are separated by spaces— these spaces, when there is no sound, are as much a part of the music as the notes themselves.

The same is true for listening. We must be very careful to not become so enamored with the words that someone says that we miss what they don't say. The music is always a combination of what is heard and what is not. When we want to Demonstrate Care, we must listen for what is said and not said. Deep listening, done well, requires several things from you:

- Be Intentional—Deep listening is not typically done quickly. Do you allow enough time to listen to those you wish to lead? Do you have one-on-one meetings in which a portion of the time is dedicated to listening? Do you conduct focus groups? Do you listen more than you talk?
- Have Patience—For me, the spaces between the notes are much harder to interpret. If you hear a particular audible note, a common refrain, you know it immediately.

However, in the silence, the messages can be much harder to discern. Deep listening requires you to recognize patterns—this will require patience.

- Show Empathy—Deep listening also requires you to enter the thoughts, feelings, and emotions of the person you are listening to. This requires your full attention; you must be fully present. Try to imagine what they are describing as if you were in their situation. Your goal is not to agree or extend sympathy—your goal is to understand completely.

Practice deep listening and you'll find it much easier to Demonstrate Care.

Pursue Real Relationships. You can Demonstrate Care for a stranger, but when you do so in the context of a relationship, it just means more. Think of an existing relationship as an opportunity to maintain and deepen care. Here are a few ideas to help pursue real relationships with those around you.

- Invest the Time—The best relationships are typically built slowly, often over years. It's not surprising for them to be a composite of many heartfelt conversations, the kind that require time. You may think, *I just don't have the time.* If you are too busy for people, you will always struggle to build meaningful relationships.
- Be Curious—I have written a lot over recent years on the value of curiosity. In *Smart Leadership*, I refer to it as a leader's fountain of youth. I stand by that claim. As it relates to relationships, curiosity may be the accelerant you throw on the fire. If someone believes you care enough

about them to be curious about their life and backstory, they will lean in.

- Be Vulnerable—This isn't the first time I've mentioned this. There is something inexplicable about the power of vulnerability. My counsel is to move slowly in this arena, but not too slowly. Sharing the truth about your hopes, dreams, fears, and challenges can accelerate and deepen a relationship.

- Stay in Touch—It's hard to have a long-term relationship if you don't have contact with someone for extended periods of time. I am not good at this! The older I get, the more I wish I had been better at this throughout my life. In the years ahead, I have promised myself to rekindle some of those past relationships I have allowed time and distance to diminish.

If you Demonstrate Care and Build Genuine Relationships with those you lead, you will have a positive impact on their lives and performance. However, former team members may provide a rich opportunity for you to practice these skills. Identify a former coworker or employee with whom you have lost touch and attempt to jump-start that relationship.

Engage Personally. There are those who would advocate for people to separate their personal life from their professional life. I disagree. First, this is an impossible expectation, and when you create an impossible expectation, you demoralize people. Second, human beings can only thrive when they are integrated. Asking someone to compartmentalize their life is asking them to bring less than their whole self to work. This lack of completeness is a form of disintegration. When something disintegrates, it is destroyed. It makes no sense to expect people to do the best work of their life if at the same time we ask them to bring only a fragment of themselves to work.

Finally, according to industrial and organizational psychologist Andrew Naber, over the course of your lifetime you will invest ninety thousand hours on the job.[4] This fact alone makes me want to engage on a personal level. This is far too much time to live devoid of real relationships.

Now, I've already shown my cards on this one: I am a raving fan of people bringing their whole self to work. This condition must be met if you are going to engage with them on a personal level. However, I want to acknowledge the inherent challenges of doing this well. Here are a few tips to help you navigate without a map.

- Honor Individual Uniqueness—The beauty and brilliance of people is their uniqueness. To honor people, get to know them. Work to understand their heart. What motivates them? What inspires them? What good do they want to do in the world? When you expend the effort to know someone at a human level, you honor them.
- Honor the Person—How do you show honor for someone? First, learn as much as you can about them. Ask them to share their story with you. Learn about their interests outside of work if they want to share that part of their story. Remember their birthday and anniversary with the organization. Give them work assignments that leverage their strengths as much as possible. Be creative and never stop trying to honor the people you lead.
- Honor the Boundaries—When I suggest engaging at a

personal level, this may set off alarm bells. Certainly, you need to respect and abide by all legal and human resource policies as established by your organization. You also need to respect the wishes of the individual. As an example, if you want to learn someone's story and they do not want to share it, you must honor their personal boundaries as well.

As we conclude this section, I want to remind you again of the importance of Valuing Results and Relationships, as well as the challenge. I know I've made the case for the significance of each of the Fundamentals—they are all essential. However, if you want to discover the full potential of your team or organization, you must embrace both results and relationships. If you overemphasize either, you will suboptimize performance over time. Regarding the challenge, remember, there is an ever-present tension when you Value both Results and Relationships. Don't try to eliminate the tension; manage it. There is power in the tension.

Your ability to Value Results and Relationships will either distinguish you as a leader or be your downfall. Remember Drucker's test of leadership: Do you get results and do you have followers? This Fundamental is the key. Don't settle for your current level of proficiency on this one. Value Results and Relationships and you'll position yourself to unlock the power and potential, and performance, of your organization and the people you serve.

VALUE RESULTS AND RELATIONSHIPS
BEST PRACTICES AND KEY STRATEGIES

Set the Example
- Know the Values
- Share the Values
- Compensate for Your Bias

Coach for Success
- Embrace the Role
- Provide Situational Coaching
- Give Great Feedback
- Praise Progress

Demonstrate Care
- Practice Deep Listening
- Pursue Real Relationships
- Engage Personally

EMBODY A LEADER'S HEART

LEAD WITH HEART

Above all else, guard your heart,
for everything you do flows from it.

KING SOLOMON

n 1863, the Civil War had been underway for almost two years. Although the war would rage on for two more years, the Union had taken sufficient land in the South for Secretary of War Edwin Stanton to declare Florida, Georgia, and South Carolina as the Department of the South. This pronouncement would ultimately create the perfect opportunity for the first woman in American history to plan and lead a military mission.[1]

Anxious to destroy plantations and liberate enslaved people who might join the fight, Colonel James Montgomery saw an opportunity to do both by orchestrating a daring nighttime attack known today as the Raid at Combahee River. The mission was bold and potentially deadly. Success would hinge on his troops' ability to navigate ten miles up the river by cover of darkness, all while avoiding the submerged mines the Confederates had placed in the river. The success of the mission and the lives of the 150-plus men were in the hands of one individual—Harriet Tubman. She, along with her team of scouts, had learned the whereabouts of the mines and coordinated how the entire venture was to unfold. This was not Harriet's first effort to assist in freeing enslaved people from the South, nor would it be her last.[2]

Tubman was born in approximately 1820 as Araminta Ross, and her parents called her Minty. Her first official act of defiance came at the age of twelve attempting to stop an overseer from abusing a fellow slave. Rather than strike the man, he struck her instead. The blow cracked her skull and the aftereffects—headaches and narcolepsy—plagued her the rest of her life.

In 1849, after hearing rumors of her and her family being sold, she escaped with two of her eight siblings. Although her brothers ultimately turned back, Minty did not. She made her way from her home in Dorchester County, Maryland, to Philadelphia—about ninety miles. After her escape, she utilized a clandestine network of safe houses and river captains known as the Underground Railroad to return home at least thirteen times over the years to lead over seventy people to freedom. She was the Railroad's most famous "conductor."[3]

When the Civil War started, Tubman served as a nurse for the Union Army for about ten months. Then, her courage and reputation gave her the opportunity to serve as a scout for the Union, during which time she learned all the details necessary to plan the daring raid up the river.

At midnight on the night of June 2, 1863, two ships entered

the river. With Harriet personally guiding the ships, the troops safely navigated the submerged explosives and made it to the Middleton plantation, which they destroyed. By the time the sun began to rise, their ships were headed out, having burned several plantations and retrieved 750 slaves.[4]

The official Confederate report summed up the encounter well:[5]

> The enemy seems to have been well posted as to the character and capacity of our troops and their small chance of encountering opposition, and to have been well guided by persons thoroughly acquainted with the river and country.

As Harriet's military successes increased, her anonymity was increasingly compromised. However, she would continue to serve the Union Army until the end of the war, often by donning a disguise as a much older woman and traveling to cities under Confederate control to learn their secrets.[6]

Throughout her life, Harriet Embodied a Leader's Heart. She was committed to lifelong learning, and this trait served her well as a spy for the North. Tubman also responded with courage time and time again in the face of unspeakable challenges. And one of her most enduring and admirable characteristics was her ever-present ability to think of others first. Her life became a living example of the power of a selfless leader.

In her postwar life, she gave generously from her meager means, often living hand to mouth. Harriet was always looking for ways to serve; she joined Susan B. Anthony in the women's

suffrage movement, and in 1896, she opened the Harriet Tubman Home for the Aged. Late in her life when asked about her
time as a conductor, Tubman said, "I never ran my train off the
track, and I never lost a passenger."[7]

All who knew Tubman could testify to her Uncommon
Greatness.

START WITH YOUR HEART

What gave Harriet the moral authority to lead others? What
gives you the authority to lead? There is a common mispercep-
tion that authority is given; it is not—real authority is earned.
Many people have a position of leadership but have no real followship. People follow leaders they trust. And they trust leaders
whose character is on full display.

In the first chapter, I mentioned a change to one of the original Fundamentals. In order to represent both leadership skills
and leadership character, I've modified the final Fundamental;
rather than Embody the Values, it is now a call to Embody a
Leader's Heart. This is a refinement, not a departure, from what
I've been teaching for many years.

For almost a quarter of a century, I have been advocating a
picture of leadership that resembles an iceberg. It is the perfect
metaphor for what makes for a successful leader. It can also be
used to illustrate why many leaders fail.

If you remember your fifth-grade science class, you know
that an iceberg is typically about 10 percent above the waterline
and about 90 percent below. The same can be said for leadership.
The 10 percent above represents your skills and the 90 percent
below represents your heart.

Skills certainly matter, and that's why so much of this book has been dedicated to some of the fundamental skills and competencies you will need to lead well. But don't miss the point—if your heart is not right, no one cares about your skills. That's why this final Fundamental feels better to me when reframed to focus on the heart. The best leaders, those pursuing Uncommon Greatness, must Embody a Leader's Heart. For many leaders, this last Fundamental is the missing piece. To become a leader people want to follow is primarily an issue of the heart. Here's a question for you to ponder: Do you overvalue leadership skills while undervaluing or overlooking the condition of your heart? If so, why? If you talk to those being led, they are crystal clear on what they value most.

We asked several thousand leaders to think about a leader who had a profound impact on their lives. We asked them to identify the reason they believed this person came to mind. Over 95 percent of those surveyed listed a character trait; less than 5 percent identified a skill or competency. The best leaders start with *their* heart before they attempt to win the hearts of others.

I'm not sure how this idea lands with you. To suggest that the best leaders start with their heart is uncommon, even countercultural, but it is not new. The late Peter Drucker is credited with saying, "The quality of character does not make the leader, but the absence flaws the entire process."[8] Both skills and the right heart are needed to be a successful leader.

What is the right heart for a successful leader? What traits, attributes, and characteristics should we work to cultivate? I wrote an entire book on this topic titled *The Heart of Leadership*. Here's a quick overview of the traits you and I need to develop and nurture throughout our lifetimes if we want to become leaders people want to follow.

Hunger for Wisdom—Have you made a commitment to lifelong learning? The best leaders have committed to growing in wisdom. Wisdom is not knowledge; knowledge is cheap and in ample supply. The phone you own has put most of the world's knowledge at your fingertips! No, leaders don't typically fail for lack of knowledge. Wisdom is a different matter. Wisdom is the ability to apply the knowledge and experience at your disposal to consistently make good decisions. And, as for this attribute of leadership character, please don't just fixate on the wisdom part. Just as important—perhaps more so—is the hunger. A Hunger for Wisdom is a condition of the heart born of the humility needed to lead well. The hunger is fueled by the desire to learn and grow. This posture reveals a teachable and humble spirit. The arrogant are not the best learners or leaders.

Expect the Best—Are you more optimistic or pessimistic? The optimistic leader will find it much easier to gain followers. If you think about this, it makes sense. Napoleon said, "Leaders are dealers in hope." How do you dispense hope if you do not believe in the promise of the future? The best leaders are certainly grounded in reality. However, they don't let their current realities steal their dreams. Good leaders have a high internal *locus of control*—a term from psychology that roughly translates to an individual's belief in their ability to affect future outcomes. If you do not believe you can rally others to create a preferred future, why are you attempting to lead? Now, if you have a natural disposition to be more of an Eeyore—the lovable, eternally pessimistic character from Winnie the Pooh—take heart! You are not destined to a life of doom and gloom. You can learn to be more optimistic and become a leader people want to follow. More ideas on this in the next chapter.

Accept Responsibility—Are you quick to take credit for the successes of your team? Not so fast! The uncommon path involves allowing others to shine and giving heartfelt praise to those closest to the work. These same leaders are also quick to Accept Responsibility when things don't work out. They embrace the idea that they are responsible for the actions and the outcomes of those they lead. This can feel strange to some. If someone else makes a mistake, shouldn't they bear responsibility for their actions? Yes and no. There are most likely two different conversations that should take place when your plans don't work. One is the private conversation in which you identify the shortcomings, missed opportunities, and missteps associated with an outcome. Then there is the conversation regarding what you, as the leader, did or did not do that contributed, directly or indirectly, to the final outcome. If something happens on your watch, you need to own it.

Respond with Courage—Are you a courageous leader? Regardless of your answer today, you can become more courageous. And you'll need to if you want to pursue Uncommon Greatness.

Virtually everything you do as a leader requires courage. Sometimes in small doses and other times in massive amounts. Examples of situations requiring it include: Who do you assign to a crucial project? When is a reorganization required? What strategies will best position your organization for the future? Which products and services should you discontinue? How do you give hard feedback to a trusted employee? Where should you invest limited capital? When do you sell a division of the company? How do you tell senior leaders the truth about your gaps and opportunities? When do you confront a poor performer? The list is endless.

For some people, Respond with Courage is a daunting trait to develop. There are those who just do not see themselves as capable of making some of these decisions. The best news: courage is like a muscle—the more you use it, the stronger it will become.

Think Others First—When I published *The Heart of Leadership*, my publisher challenged me to arrange the heart habits in order of priority. I took his advice and decided to begin that book with Think Others First. As you consider the attributes of a leader's heart, this is first among equals.

People want to follow leaders who have the interest of others at heart. The ability to look at a situation and divorce yourself from the consequences or personal sacrifice required is the defining attribute of the leaders we love the most. These women and men truly have the best interests of others at the forefront of their thinking and their actions.

Based on our research, I realize that to Think Others First may not be your first instinct. When we asked leaders to identify the factors impeding the effectiveness of their immediate supervisor, we learned that ego was the most prevalent. Forty-six percent of employees indicated that their supervisor demonstrated egotistical behaviors. Be careful on this one!

To keep your ego in check, here's a quick to-do list for your consideration: seek feedback, listen deeply, keep learning, stop comparing, and be honest with yourself about your real strengths and weaknesses.

BE, KNOW, DO

In 1960, a small group of young girls were gathered for what might have been their last meeting; their troop leader had resigned. These future leaders were continuing a tradition that began in 1912 when Juliette Gordon Low gathered another group of girls in Savannah, Georgia. Low wanted to help the girls grow their character, fitness, and service to others. This was the beginning of the Girl Scouts.

To keep the group from disbanding, Frances Hesselbein agreed to fill in until a proper leader could be found. Frances went on to do far more than fill in. After serving as a volunteer for sixteen years, she was asked to interview to become CEO of the Girls Scouts of America. She didn't think she would get the job and by her own admission was extremely candid during the interview. She told the board they needed a "radical transformation to be relevant." In forty-eight hours, she was offered the job and accepted. Hesselbein was the CEO of the Girl Scouts of America from 1976 to 1990.[9]

During her tenure, the organization flourished. Membership grew by more than 30 percent to almost three million girls, volunteers numbered more than 750,000, and their financial stability was restored under her leadership. Hesselbein recast the mission to raise up a generation of strong and confident leaders. Her focus: courage, confidence, and character development. She also expanded the organization's global influence and pioneered diversity and inclusion efforts.

One of Hesselbein's books, *Be, Know, Do*, was co-authored with Eric Shinseki, the retired four-star general and former Chief of Staff for the U.S. Army. They articulate the significance of these three critical activities for every leader:[10]

1. **Be**—This first tenet focuses on who the leader is at their core. I suggest this is an issue of the heart. Hesselbein says, "Leadership is a matter of how to be, not how to do." This belief that leadership is more about the person than it is about position led her to ban words that indicated a hierarchical relationship like *up* and *down*.

2. **Know**—The importance of a leader possessing the skills and competence to lead well. Two years into the Scouts' transformation, Hesselbein realized her leaders needed a bigger vision for the impact they could have on the

world. She partnered with the Harvard Business School to create a program for her executives. The course was catalytic and sparked tremendous growth for the people and the organization.

3. **Do**—The critical role of action in determining a leader's efficacy. Hesselbein wanted to do her best and bring the best to bear for her organization. When the team needed a new logo, she hired the legendary designer Saul Bass to create their new mark. She also enlisted the help of John Creedon, former president of MetLife, to help with fundraising. Hesselbein believed that whatever you do, you must do with excellence.

As our team worked on this section of the book, we were challenged finding examples and illustrations to bring the idea of Embody a Leader's Heart to life. This challenge was not born from a lack of examples but that many of these examples were, frankly, more common in their appearance. The leaders we studied did what they needed to do, often with little or no fanfare. Along the way, you could see glimpses of the heart that motivated their behaviors. In Hesselbein's case, one of those revealing moments occurred when then-president Ronald Reagan invited her to join his cabinet. As important as the work would have been for the president and our nation, not to mention the added visibility Hesselbein would garner, she decided to decline his offer and continue to serve her girls; this was her calling.

After leaving the Girl Scouts, Hesselbein was recruited to lead the Peter Drucker Foundation for Nonprofit Management; Drucker had been her friend and mentor for many years.

Determined to continue to serve, Hesselbein also joined several boards and wrote multiple influential books on leadership. She received the Presidential Medal of Freedom, the United States' highest civilian award, from President Bill Clinton in 1998.[11]

Hesselbein was still serving as the CEO of the Drucker Foundation at the age of 104, although it had been renamed in her honor in 2012. The new name: the Frances Hesselbein Leadership Institute. When interviewed by Robert Reiss for *Forbes* during the pandemic in 2022, she was the oldest active CEO in America. During that conversation, she assured the world that we would get through the pandemic (she had firsthand experience with the 1918 flu pandemic). When asked about her long-standing tenure, she answered, "Age is irrelevant, it is what you do with your life that matters."[12]

What fueled this iconic leader and thrust her into a life of influence on a global stage? Perhaps we can find a clue in the fact that she saw leadership as her calling and her life's motto was "To serve is to live." What a fitting way to summarize a life and the heart of a quintessential Uncommon Leader.

BEST LEADERSHIP ADVICE?

Have you ever been part of a tweet chat? I had not, but my team suggested I participate in one. I had a lot of questions. Here's how they described the experience.

"We'll go live on Twitter and a host will send you a question. You'll respond, and we'll post your response. Then, those in the Twittersphere will respond to your response."

"Is that it?" I asked.

"Well, then we repeat the process every five minutes."

"For how long?"

"For an hour."

With some uncertainty, I said yes.

When we started this chat adventure, at first the responses to my answers came in at a manageable pace. Then, someone with hundreds of thousands of followers joined our chat. The responses were scrolling by so fast it was impossible to read them all. Fifty-five minutes in, I was exhausted mentally and physically. There was only one more question. "What is the best leadership advice you've ever received?" Nothing like ending with an easy question!

For those who are not familiar with the mechanics of Twitter, my answer needed to be very succinct—my team had advised me to keep my responses to about one hundred characters. Let's hit PAUSE here. How would you answer that question? It is a good one to reflect on. Here's what I said:

Above all else, guard your heart, for everything you do flows from it.

I still don't believe I've ever received any better leadership advice. Some of you may be wondering where I picked up this nugget. It's ancient wisdom from King Solomon, who lived almost three thousand years ago.

Remember in the introduction when I promised you nothing more than the truth? This final Fundamental is another opportunity to make good on my promise. The single biggest factor that will determine your leadership efficacy, influence, and impact over time is your heart. If your heart is not right, no one cares about your skills.

Try This: Consider starting a Leadership Development Group. Make a list of five to eight leaders or aspiring leaders who might join you. Go to LeadEveryDay.com and click on the Groups tab. You'll find FREE resources there to help you get started—tips, best practices, recommended books to study, and FREE study questions. I've been in a group like this for over twenty-five years. Trust me, you'll never regret locking arms with others who will help you grow as a leader.

EMBODY
A LEADER'S HEART:
IDEAS FOR ACTION

Leaders are different. They see the world differently. They think differently. They respond differently to life's daily challenges. Much of this difference can be traced back to their heart. In ancient times, conventional wisdom was that the heart was the seat of all behavior and emotions. Although we know that, scientifically, this is not the case, there is something poetic about the centrality of the heart.

This chapter is organized around the five heart habits that enable us to move from common to Uncommon Leadership: **Hunger for Wisdom**, **Expect the Best**, **Accept Responsibility**, **Respond with Courage**, and **Think Others First**. As with previous Ideas for Action chapters, you'll find many tactical ideas on how to activate these best practices in your life and leadership. Cultivate each of these and you will become a leader people want to follow.

HUNGER FOR WISDOM

The best leaders are learners, period. It is their voracious, insatiable desire to learn and grow that enables them to serve well over the long haul. One of the defining moments in my life was when a leader helped me understand that my capacity to grow would determine my capacity to lead. Thankfully for me, this was over four decades ago. I'm still learning. If you haven't yet committed to lifelong learning, join me! It's a decision you will never regret. Here are some ideas to help you on your journey.

Create a Development Plan. Leaders who want to launch or grow an existing business have a plan. Leaders who want to ensure a comfortable retirement have a financial plan. Leaders who want to address a significant challenge in their organization's culture have a plan. A general about to go into battle creates a plan. The leaders of the D-Day attack that ultimately led to the end of World War II had a plan that took two years to complete.[1] Generally speaking, leaders understand the power and purpose of a well-conceived plan. However, most of the leaders I know do not have a plan for their personal growth and development. I encourage you to create a personal development plan. Here are a few tips to help you get started or refine what you have already begun.

- Don't Get Caught in the One-Size-Fits-All Mentality—I have seen very effective plans that were pages long and others that were less than a single page. You can even draw it on a napkin if you would like. The plan is a tool for *you*. What will help you learn and grow in the coming months?

- Create an Annual Plan—You can do a weekly, monthly, annual, or a five-year plan. I've been creating an annual personal development plan for decades—a one-year plan works for me. This time horizon gives me enough time to go deep on a topic and have ample opportunity for application, reflection, and practice.

- Keep the Plan Focused—Select a few items you would like to concentrate on over the coming months. If you do, you are much more likely to see improvement. Be specific. As a communicator, the topics of adult learning and storytelling have been my choices in different years.

- Put Your Plan in Writing and Be Specific—My life coach told me that only one thing happens when you create a written and specific plan: you accomplish more of your plan.

- Review Your Plan Often—As I reflect on the many years I've been practicing this discipline, I think the single greatest factor in the years in which I have learned and grown the most is the frequency with which I review my plan. These days, I review a plan summary daily—it helps me stay focused.

- Share Your Plan with Others—Accountability is a gift that encourages you to do what you have decided you want to do. Who can you share your plan with? I have nine guys I share my plan with every year. It helps!

Learn Every Day. I meet far too many leaders who think learning and development is extracurricular. I have heard some version of the following countless times: "I just don't have time to learn and grow as a leader." These leaders think of personal growth as a nice-to-do versus a necessity. Tragically, these leaders will never reach their full potential.

Leaders who have chosen this mindset have decided to limit their impact. Learning needs to become a lifestyle, a worldview, and a significant part of your identity as a leader. How do you do that? Well, the options are infinite, but let's make it simple: learn something every day.

Some of you are thinking, *Can I really learn something every day?* You did when you were younger. I enjoy asking my grand-kids, "What did you learn at school today?" They always have an answer!

For the next two weeks, at the end of every day, ask your-self, "What did I learn today, if anything?" Write down your response. Ask yourself what was different on the days you did or did not learn anything. My guess is that with less effort than you probably expect, you can embrace the personal leadership discipline to learn something every day.

Pay It Forward. Make a commitment to share what you are learning with others. This single idea will create a positive ripple effect in your sphere of influence. I call this strategy "pay it forward." As I think back on my life and career, I'm thankful for leaders that not only did this for me and my coworkers but encouraged me to do the same for those around me.

Why would pay it forward be an idea under the strategy of Hunger for Wisdom? Three reasons.

When you know that you are going to share what you are learning, you pay attention more. In essence, the decision to share with others forces you to have something to share. Here's what marketing guru and thought leader Seth Godin says about his decision to post online content daily:[2]

If you know you have to write a blog post tomorrow, something in writing, something that will be around six months from now, about something in the world, you will start looking for something in the world to write about. You will seek to notice something interesting and to say something creative about it.

Sharing what you are learning models a teachable and humble spirit. Insecure leaders are far less vulnerable with what they are learning and areas in which they are trying to grow. The act of sharing also normalizes the priority of personal growth.

Sharing your learnings with others accelerates their growth. You may say, "You should definitely read this book." Or, you may say, "Here's what I learned from the book . . ." In this case, you may have transferred sufficient knowledge and information such that they no longer need to read the book. They received the benefit of your effort. You served them in that moment and likely saved them hours of time.

EXPECT THE BEST

Remember, according to Napoleon, "Leaders are dealers in hope." I don't think you have to believe the general on this one. You can trust from your own experience that we expect an optimistic tone from those we choose to follow. Here's how you can begin to cultivate this crucial leadership trait.

Learn to Be Optimistic. Optimistic people are statistically proven to live longer, healthier, happier lives than pessimists. What's more is that optimists are often more successful as well. One study, explored by Martin E. P. Seligman, PhD, in his book

Learned Optimism, tested this theory with MetLife's insurance sales force. Those individuals who scored high on their ASQ (a test designed to unearth natural optimism vs. pessimism) sold 37 percent more than their pessimist counterparts.[3]

As a leader, part of your job is to inspire hope, gain followship, and Build Trust with your employees. If you are telling yourself how poor of a leader you are, there is no doubt this belief will manifest itself in your leadership. Optimism is essential to build strong beliefs in yourself and inspire others through an optimistic lens.

Here's an abbreviated version of Seligman's approach. The next time you face a situation, break it down into the ABCs:

- What is the Adversity you are facing?
- What are your Beliefs about the situation?
- What are the Consequences if you keep those beliefs?

If your beliefs are filled with negative sentiment and cause consequences that are harmful, try reframing those beliefs to something more neutral or positive. Over time, you will naturally build your optimism and, as a consequence, you'll lead more effectively.

Although the best leaders have an optimistic outlook on the future, this should not be confused with a distorted view of the present. Never settle for anything less than the truth; do everything in your power to discover it.

Remember Your Wins. To move with confidence into an unknown future can be challenging. As leaders, there is so much we really don't know. What obstacles will we encounter? How will our people respond? Will I be up to the challenge? Will others follow my lead? Will we find begrudging complacence or wholehearted commitment to the vision? The list of questions is endless. However, we must lead. One source of strength and courage is to remember your wins.

For most leaders, their next challenge will not be their first. Even if it is, you likely have a deep well of personal accomplishments to draw upon. Reflect on past circumstances, conflicts, and challenges. What did you learn? How did you grow? What can you extrapolate from your past victories?

Make a list. Get out your computer or a piece of paper and list as many of your past wins as you can think of in ten minutes. Don't focus on just the big ones, like landing a new job (this counts for sure, but remember the smaller wins too), hiring a talented new team member, landing a new account, solving a significant problem, and so on.

Now, step two: take your list and type or write down one thing you learned from each of these wins. If you have any doubt about your ability to lead into an unknown future, you may need to do this often. Some leaders do this type of reflection daily. Regardless of the frequency or your methodology, I think it's a good idea to remember your wins.

Visualize Success. What does it look like to Expect the Best? Do you have a crystal-clear picture of what success looks like? If you cannot see what you are pursuing, then where are you headed? High achievers in many fields have discovered the power unleashed when they visualize success.

Over the years, visualization has steadily gotten more popular, but it is not a new concept; in fact, nearly every elite athlete you can think of has been using the technique for decades. World champion golfer Jack Nicklaus said this about his work on the course: "I never hit a shot, not even in practice, without having a very sharp, in-focus picture of it in my head. It's like a color movie. First I 'see' where I want it to finish, nice and white and sitting up high on the bright green grass. Then the scene quickly changes and I 'see' the ball going there: its path, trajectory, and shape, even its behavior on landing. Then there is this sort of fadeout, and the next scene shows me making the kind of swing that will turn the previous images to reality."[4]

Jack is not alone either. Sports psychologists across the globe use visualization as one of their primary tools to help prepare the best athletes in the world for their moment in the spotlight. Michael Phelps's coach, Bob Bowman, made him practice visualizing a successful race as a strict part of his training routine, every night before bed and right when he woke up.[5] When you visualize, you are activating the same parts of the brain that are active when you engage in that activity.

How could this practice serve you as you work to Expect the Best? Before you begin your next project or make your next big presentation or have a challenging conversation with a member of your team—stop and just imagine what it is going to feel like and look like to succeed. Use as many senses as you can.

While nothing will ever replace the live, in-the-moment experience, you will likely learn that mental rehearsals and visualization will help you build both your skill and your confidence.

ACCEPT RESPONSIBILITY

The "Buck Stops Here" was the sign on President Harry S. Truman's desk. It was a constant reminder that the leader should not pass blame to others. I believe every leader needs a sign like this—if not physically on our desks, at least emblazoned on our hearts and minds. Here are a few tactics to help you embrace this important mindset and practice.

Do Your Job. Bill Belichick, the legendary coach of the New England Patriots, has made "Do your job" more than a mantra—this single phrase encompasses much of his philosophy as a successful coach in the highly competitive National Football League. Belichick understands the importance of the team. Unless everyone does his specific task as assigned, the plays don't work, the points aren't scored, and the team doesn't win. As leaders in a complex world, we are playing a team sport as well. And while it is easy for leaders to tell others to do their job, this behavior must begin with the leader.[6]

Role clarity should always precede goal clarity. One of the most important things you can do as a leader is to establish complete clarity on key roles and responsibilities for you and your team. Then, once these roles are clear, stay in your lane. One of the roles you must own is the responsibility for the outcomes of your team. In an ideal world, the team is accountable for the work itself, but if the outcomes are not what you expected, you must own this. This should not be a passive ownership, resulting in thinking, *Oh well, things just didn't work out as we planned.* No, your role is to acknowledge the shortcoming, claim responsibility, and go to work to help the team prevent similar outcomes in the future.

You need to help the team with things they cannot do for themselves—you, as the leader, have a unique role. Typically, teams need their leader to set vision, provide boundaries, secure the needed resources, and more. These are things only you can do.

Make a list of the Top Ten things you should own in your role. I gave you a head start in the previous paragraph. If you want bonus points, make a list of the Top Ten activities or responsibilities the team must own.

Admit Your Mistakes. You may have heard the ancient proverb "pride goes before a fall." It's true. Leaders who will not admit their mistakes are at great risk. Their job may not be on the line, but their leadership is. There hasn't been enough written about *followership*, but every leader should care deeply about this concept. The essence of the idea is that followers decide who they will follow. Now, if those you seek to lead decide not to follow you, that doesn't mean they are going to quit—they might, but more likely they will begin to comply rather than commit. They will do the minimum, not the maximum. Discretionary effort will cease to exist. Loss of creativity, innovation, and imagination will be close behind.

How do you avoid compliance behavior and instead build followership? The full answer is much bigger than we can address here. However, a great place to start is to admit your mistakes. You may be the leader, but you are still human. You do make mistakes, and your team knows it. Assuming you don't make too many mistakes (at some point your competency will be called into question), your vulnerability in admitting your shortcomings and missteps will actually strengthen your leadership. I know it is counterintuitive.

Brené Brown has researched the topic of vulnerability and leadership for years and has concluded, "Vulnerability is the core of shame and fear and our struggle for worthiness. But it is also the birthplace of joy, creativity, belonging, and love."[7]

It may feel strange, but when you blow it, admit your

mistakes—your stock will rise in the hearts and minds of those you lead.

Give Praise Freely. This next idea may strike you as an odd tactic under the heading of Accept Responsibility. While I stand by everything I've said in the previous pages and I wholeheartedly believe the buck stops with the leader, acknowledging the contributions of others is huge.

Imagine the leader who accepts all the credit for the accomplishments of the team. Chances are high they are not a serving leader, but rather, most likely, a self-serving leader. By offering genuine recognition of the accomplishments and contributions of others, we can take a step to becoming the leader people want to follow.

Find someone on your team or in your organization you can recognize this week. Make the moment personal and specific. Work to make this type of behavior second nature. The truth is your team does most of the day-to-day work. Try not to forget that.

RESPOND WITH COURAGE

Courage is the catalyst for all true leadership and an elemental component of Uncommon Greatness. For some of you, courage is not a felt need—you were blessed with it in abundance, or you forged it over time. For others, it is a daily challenge. Regardless of where you are on this continuum today, the more influence you seek and the more impact you want to have on the world, the more courage you're going to need. I believe you'll find some ideas here to serve you as you work to become a more courageous leader.

Acknowledge Your Fears. Fear is not an emotion to be banished but is a fuel source to be harnessed. The real heroes in our world are not those without fear; they are the ones who move beyond their fears. Fears come in all shapes and sizes. Some, to an outsider, might seem trivial, while others are so disempowering they can immobilize you. I'm not a therapist and don't want to pretend I am. However, I do know that to acknowledge your fear—to name it, to write it down, to even say it out loud if we dare—can be liberating for many. Often the mere act of owning our fears can provide the courage to overcome them.

Another benefit of working through the process of identifying our specific fears before they surface is the opportunity this provides to predetermine what we will do when they surface. In his book *Never Finished*, David Goggins talks about how knowing that he feared water *before* he entered the surf during the Navy SEALs Hell Week enabled him to decide in advance how he would respond when the inevitable happened—SEALs get in the water. He had already foreshadowed how he would feel if he let his fears overtake him. He played the movie of his life forward if he quit the SEALs program and did not like what he believed would happen to his life if he let his fears dictate his actions. In the crucible, he called upon his own agency when the cold waves of the Pacific pummeled his body; he overcame his fears, at least for the moment, survived the water, and became a SEAL. As far as I know from Goggins's social posts, he still doesn't like the water.[8]

Make two lists. First, list the things you are afraid of in life (e.g., public speaking, death, appearing to be incompetent, fear of failure, etc.). Next, look at your calendar for the next week. Are there any upcoming activities that stir fear, or its younger brother, anxiety, on your schedule (e.g., a presentation to the board, a hard conversation with an employee, etc.)? Armed with these two lists, ask yourself: *What can I do to reduce or at least mitigate these fears?* In most every situation, there will be something you can do to lower your stress, anxiety, and fear.

Fail Forward. Failure is part of life and leadership. To deny this is to deny reality. John Maxwell says, "Changing your perspective on failure will help you to persevere—and ultimately achieve your desires."[9]

One of my mentors challenged me not to deliberate on my decision too long. When I probed, he said this: "No matter how long you deliberate, there will come a point when additional information will not help you. Besides, 50 percent of your decisions will be wrong regardless." I was shocked by that statistic. Then he added, "If you spend half your time trying to make good decisions, you'll invest the other half of your time and energy making the decisions you missed right."

Wow! I'm not sure the 50/50 spilt is scientifically derived, but I do know this: leaders are going to fail. Sometimes in epic fashion, often publicly, but in countless other situations, our failures will be small and inconsequential in the greater scheme of things. For you and me, the question is not how we avoid the inevitable but rather, how do we make our bad decisions good? How do we fail forward? Here are a few tips to help:

- Name the Failure—We already covered this earlier in Accept Responsibility. Your opportunity for deep learning and future success hinges on this first step.
- Identify the Root Causes—If you want to learn from your mistakes, you must do the hard, often time-consuming

work of figuring out what really happened and why. Note: rarely is the presenting problem the root cause.

- Document What You Learned—Many problems resurface, sometimes in their previous form but often masquerading as something new and novel. Take good notes and try not to make the same mistake twice.

Stretch Yourself. Courage is built like a muscle. Many small movements over time will build strength. However, sometimes intentionally taking a big step out of your comfort zone can pay huge dividends. Sometimes, it's helpful to stretch yourself. Accept the challenge to do something big. It may not be big for others, but for you, it would require bold action and courage.

When you try this, you determine your success metrics—don't let others do that for you. If you choose wisely and set your own standard of measurement, you can use this technique to make big deposits in your courage account.

My oldest son, Justin, and I established a practice years ago of attempting something every year that would stretch us. Our challenges have ranged from scuba diving (remember, what challenges me may not be a challenge for you—I, like Goggins, really, really don't like water) to climbing some of the world's highest peaks. But the craziest thing I think we ever did was run a marathon.

Now, I'm sure many of you have run a marathon. But when Justin came up with this idea, I hadn't run to the mailbox since I was in my twenties. However, we committed, and we did it. It stretched me! People often ask about my race time. I'm not ashamed of my time, but my goal was not a time-bound goal; my goal was to finish. By setting the finish line as the goal, I knew my odds of success went up drastically. Unless they took me off the course on a stretcher, I *would* finish. When you stretch yourself, set your own success metrics. For the purposes of building courage, the attempt is more valuable than the accomplishment.

If you want to jump-start your efforts to be more courageous, or just accelerate your development, try something hard, something difficult, something that will stretch you. It doesn't have to be a mountain or a race. Go back to school, take the bar exam, start a nonprofit, or launch a side hustle. When you do things that stretch you, win or lose, you will flex your courage muscles. (BTW, we finished the marathon in five hours and nineteen minutes.)

THINK OTHERS FIRST

I shared in the previous chapter my belief that Think Others First is the most important of the five heart habits we've explored on the previous pages. I'll take that a step further—I think it is foundational for the pursuit of Uncommon Greatness.

Leaders who cannot cultivate a Think Others First mindset will be forever excluded from the ranks of truly great leaders. They, with a lot of effort, will hit the glass ceiling of common greatness. Most of them will never know why they are unfulfilled and dissatisfied with their lives and leadership despite their accomplishments. Even if you have this part of leadership mastered, please take good notes. We are now talking about the cornerstone you can both use and share with others who seek a life of profound impact. Here are some ideas to help you as you strive to always Think Others First.

Add Value. How many people are in your sphere of

influence? If I asked you to make a list, most of you would probably draw a relatively small circle. In his best-selling book *The Tipping Point*, Malcolm Gladwell says that most of us have a social network of thirty-five to fifty people. He reached this conclusion using a standardized test in which an individual selects from a list of 250 surnames. Your score is how many of the names match someone you know. If you score more than seventy, Gladwell will consider you a highly social connector. This may be the number of people you know personally, but this is not the limit of your influence.[10]

Just imagine how many people we interact with over the course of our lifetimes—the clerk at the convenience store, the stranger we open the door for, the people we pass on the sidewalk, the coworkers we pass in the hallway or share Zoom calls with. I don't even know how to calculate this number. The potential for impact is tremendous.

Here's my challenge for you: try to add value to every person you encounter. Let that sink in for a moment before you react. Now, the more pragmatic and realistic among you are probably thinking, *That's impossible!*

Notice my choice of words: "*Try* to add value . . ." Does that emphasis change your reaction? If you want to Think Others First, you must shift your focus off yourself and on to other people. If you are trying to add value to someone, who are you thinking about? Them, of course. It is the attempt to add value that changes you regardless of your success rate.

How do you add value to someone else? I want you to make a list. I think you'll be surprised how many ideas you can come up with. Here are a few to get you started:

- Encourage them.
- Recognize them.
- Coach them.
- Correct them.
- Empathize with their situation.
- Ask their opinion.
- Offer a genuine compliment.
- Thank them.
- Acknowledge their strengths.
- Offer a silent prayer on their behalf if you are a person of faith.
- Be present during a challenging life circumstance—just show up.
- Share a smile—a simple gesture that can lift someone's spirits.
- Provide resources (a podcast, a book recommendation; in some cases, you can provide tangible resources like a gift card to a local restaurant for the person experiencing homelessness).

For the next week, try to add value to everyone you meet. I want to hear from you. How did it go? How did you feel? How did others react? What did you attempt that is not on my list above? Please email me your experience at Mark@LeadEveryDay.com.

Listen to Understand. How good are you at listening? The statistics on this are sobering. In a survey of 14,000 employees, only 8 percent indicated that their mid-level and senior leaders listened "very well."[11] We, meaning 92 percent of us, need to work on this. To Think Others First becomes exceedingly difficult if we cannot hear them. I believe the best leaders are the best listeners. Slow down and Listen to Understand. Here are a few ideas to help you listen well:

- Be Proactive—How much time do you dedicate to listening? Look at your calendar for the last thirty days. How much time do you devote to this critical activity beyond your normal routine (e.g., listening in meetings)?
- Be Strategic—If you decide you need to ramp up your Listening to Understand activities, identify the priority groups in your world (customers, employees, board members, peers, etc.). Schedule time for some listening conversations with these people.
- Ask Better Questions—What are you listening for? Here's a short list of questions to stimulate your thinking. When you learn your people's answers to these questions and others like them, you'll begin to understand them at a deeper level.

What are your hopes and dreams?
What gives you energy?
What type of activities drain you?
What are your strengths?
What's the best recognition you ever received?
What does your ideal day away from work look like?
What does a great day at work look like?
How can I serve you?

If the people you lead were asked to rate your listening, what would they say? You may want to ask them. If your organization conducts an employee survey, consider asking a "listening question" to establish the scope of your opportunity. Also, regardless of how you are evaluated, take heart. You do have to start where you are, but you do not have to stay there.

Lead with Empathy. How empathetic are you as a human being? For us as leaders, this is either a huge asset or liability depending on how much empathy we can muster in a given situation. Let's be sure we are clear on terminology here. When I say *empathy*, I am referring to our ability to enter another person's situation and circumstance at an emotional level and feel what they are feeling.

If this is not a natural strength for you, here are a few things you can do to be more empathetic.

- Slow Down—It's impossible to demonstrate "drive-by" empathy. Do you have time to fully engage in the emotions of another human being? Certainly not for everyone you know, but are there people for whom you should slow down from time to time? I think so. How about your family? Close friends? Your staff? Are you mentoring anyone right now? They need more than your sage wisdom—they need you to understand their situation. Who else comes to mind?
- Repeat What You Hear—There is something comforting in knowing that we have been seen and heard as human beings. Repeat back what the person speaking to you has said so they know you understood. Also, when we attempt to play back what we are hearing, it puts added pressure on us to listen well.
- Don't Try to Solve Every Problem—For leaders, this can

be a challenge. I remember a team member years ago who needed a listening ear. She knew me well, so before she started telling me her story, she said, "I don't need you to solve anything for me. I just need you to listen." What she didn't say, but I understood completely, was that she was hoping I would listen intently and understand her situation at a deep and personal level. For me, this story is a good reminder—although leaders spend much of our lives solving problems, this is not a demand imposed by empathy.

As we come to the end of this last Fundamental and the ideas to help you become a leader people want to follow, I feel like my closing comments throughout the book have reflected a theme. As I've closed the previous Ideas for Action chapters, I shared why I believe each one is essential as you attempt to practice Uncommon Leadership. Here we are again.

As you consider the priority a leader must give this final Fundamental, make no mistake: to Embody a Leader's Heart is the *real* game changer. The majority of your influence will not be determined by your level of mastery of the first four Fundamentals. Remember the iceberg—90 percent is unseen to the casual observer.

In our research we confirmed the obvious—people want to work with and for leaders who know how to lead. However, the skill set of the leader was not the most important factor in gaining followship. The heart of the leader matters more. I believe virtually everyone who has worked in an organizational setting can identify someone who appeared to have the skills of leadership yet no one wanted to follow them. Your heart matters more than you may want to admit.

Please do not write off this heart stuff as soft. If you do, you will severely limit your future influence and impact. Anything you are able to accomplish without a leader's heart will be a hollow victory and a mere fraction of what you could have accomplished. If your heart is not right, no one cares about your skills. Above all else, guard your heart!

EMBODY A LEADER'S HEART
BEST PRACTICES AND KEY STRATEGIES

Hunger for Wisdom
- Create a Development Plan
- Learn Every Day
- Pay It Forward

Expect the Best
- Learn to Be Optimistic
- Remember Your Wins
- Visualize Success

Accept Responsibility
- Do Your Job
- Admit Your Mistakes
- Give Praise Freely

Respond with Courage
- Acknowledge Your Fears
- Fail Forward
- Stretch Yourself

Think Others First
- Add Value
- Listen to Understand
- Lead with Empathy

EPILOGUE: ALWAYS SERVE

The great leader is seen as a servant first,
and that simple fact is the key to his greatness.

ROBERT GREENLEAF

I n the fall of 1978, I was out of work, having just been laid off after only six months on the job. I was young and foolish, but I had enough sense to know I needed a job. That's when I decided to apply for a position at the Chick-fil-A home office. I had done a relatively short stint as a team member in one of their local restaurants (that didn't go well). However, for some inexplicable reason, I thought perhaps I could work at the company's corporate headquarters. Even as I write this, I am once again reminded how crazy this idea was. However, I went in and told the receptionist I wanted a job working in their warehouse. She asked me to take a seat. I thought to myself, *Okay, that's a good sign; she didn't tell me to leave.*

A few minutes later, Truett Cathy, the founder of Chick-fil-A, came out and greeted me. He invited me into his office to conduct the interview. If this sounds odd to you, it felt odd to me! *Why is the CEO interviewing a kid to work in the warehouse?*

I didn't immediately know the answer to my question. However, after a very short interview, Truett said, "Well, someone in the warehouse quit yesterday . . . I guess you can have the job." It was only later I understood why *he* was conducting the interview. In 1978, the Chick-fil-A home office employed only fifteen people—I would be the sixteenth.

WHO ARE YOUR HEROES?

The Fundamentals this book is based on, and their accompanying practices, have been informed by countless voices. On the previous pages, you heard from a tiny fraction of those contributors. However, I thought it would be a fitting close to this book to show you what it looks like when all these Fundamentals converge and are embodied in a single individual. I've said for many years, we all need role models. Leaders we can look up to, learn from, and emulate. We all need real-life leadership heroes, and Truett Cathy was one of mine. Let's look at how the Fundamentals of Uncommon Leadership manifested themselves in his life and leadership.

See the Future—Truett was a visionary leader. Many people know about the growth of Chick-fil-A from a single restaurant opened in 1946 to a $20 billion enterprise and still growing. What most do not know are some of Truett's lesser-known efforts to create a better tomorrow. One example comes immediately to mind: Truett's desire to help young people have a better future.

In 1955, Truett had just one restaurant, and one of his employees, Eddie White, wanted to go to college. At the time, Eddie was serving as a grill man and butcher for Truett. To raise support for his dream, Eddie put a jar on the counter with a handwritten label: "Eddie's College Fund." When the day came for Eddie to make the first payment to Morehouse College, there was not enough in the jar. Truett gladly stepped in and made up the difference. He also sent Eddie to a local department store to purchase new clothes for his pending departure.

Eddie went to the store under protest to satisfy his boss. When he arrived, he told the salesman he didn't really need any clothes, to which the salesman replied, "Mr. Cathy wants you to get a new suit, shirt, shoes, and proper undergarments. He is paying for everything."

After graduating from college, Eddie went on to become an educator and assistant superintendent in the Atlanta public school system. They even named a school after him.

Long before Truett was a wealthy man, he could see the potential in people and wanted to be part of their future success. Sometimes his support was financial, other times an encouraging word, or perhaps coaching along the way. I benefited from all of the above.

Eddie's experience foreshadowed Truett's commitment to providing opportunities for his employees to pursue higher education. In the years since Truett gave that first scholarship to Eddie, the organization has helped over one hundred thousand Team Members pursue their academic goals by awarding almost

$200 million in scholarships. I received the scholarship myself. Thanks, Truett!

Engage and Develop Others—Jimmy Collins was Truett's third employee at the Chick-fil-A home office (today it's called the Support Center). Jimmy went on to become the president of the company and served the organization for more than thirty years. Before his retirement, he loved to tell this story about Truett:

Truett and Jimmy were at a grand opening of an early restaurant. They noticed a team member working one of the registers was not smiling as she greeted and served the guests. Jimmy said to Truett, "I'll take care of this." He went over to the woman and said, "You need to smile while serving the guests." Jimmy rejoined Truett, and they continued to watch the activity at the front counter. A few minutes later, Truett made the observation that the team member was still not smiling. Jimmy said, "I got this." He went back to the team member and said, "You have got to smile." Thinking his mission complete, he returned to Truett's side.

A few minutes later, in the midst of all the hustle and bustle of the grand opening, Truett pointed out to Jimmy again that the young woman was still not smiling. Jimmy said he would handle it and Truett stopped him. "Let me talk to her."

Truett approached the young lady and said, "I've noticed you have a wonderful smile." The girl beamed. "Thank you, sir." Truett's response: "I think our guests would enjoy seeing it as much as I do." You guessed it, she offered a genuine and joyful smile to every guest she served for the rest of her shift.

Truett just had a way with people that is hard to explain. He was also the business guy who would negotiate hard on prices. He was known to go from one counter to another at the airport to negotiate the best deal on a rental car. I was even with him once when he attempted to get a senior citizen discount from an airport vendor on a pack of gum. His frugality was perhaps a byproduct of growing up during the Great Depression. Yet, the counterbalance was his radical generosity. I've never known a more generous person. Not just with the financial resources, but also with his time, encouragement, instruction, and love.

Reinvent Continuously—When I think about this Fundamental, countless examples from Truett's life come to mind, but none can surpass the invention of the chicken sandwich.

In the early 1960s, Truett was operating his original restaurant, a short-order grill that he and his brother had opened in 1946 not far from the Atlanta airport and Ford assembly plant. The proximity to these businesses allowed him to operate his restaurant twenty-four hours a day. His customers wanted their food fast—many had only a short break for their meals. After continued frustration with how long it took to cook the fried chicken, Truett began to experiment. He wanted to reinvent the way he cooked chicken. This pursuit quickly led to the idea of fileting the chicken and pressure-cooking the breast. He discovered this process was much faster and yielded a moist and flavorful product. From there it was a short step to serving the filet on a bun. The Chick-fil-A sandwich was born!

One more example of Truett's ability to practice this Fundamental is the way the deal is structured with the people who operate the restaurants. Truett's insight was the realization that successful businesses had two elemental components: capital and management (leadership). He realized the pool of people who had both was relatively small. However, the number of people with the leadership acumen and the desire to run their own business was huge. Therefore, his model was built on the company providing the capital and finding the people who could operate the restaurants. All that is required even today is a $10,000 investment on the part of the Operator. For many decades, there was only a $5,000 refundable deposit required.

Truett's instincts were correct. This unique arrangement produces exceptional results, a ready supply of high-caliber candidates, and extremely high retention. (For decades, Operator retention has hovered around 95 percent.) Tens of thousands of inquiries are submitted annually from individuals who want to be in business *for* themselves but not *by* themselves. The organization has been able to attract some amazing leaders, many of whom would not have been able to provide their own capital.

Value Results and Relationships—In my opinion, this was one of Truett's greatest strengths. I don't know that I've ever known a leader who appeared to Value both Results and Relationships so naturally. In Truett's case, his ability to live in and manage the tension appeared effortless. From my vantage point, he always cared about the people *and* the results. He was simultaneously a caring and compassionate human being and a pragmatic businessperson.

When I was serving as a leader on our Field Operations team, I had to brief Truett from time to time on any performance issues or concerns with the restaurant Operators. After one of these briefings, Truett reminded me my job was not merely to terminate the poor performers. As I recall the conversation, he said, "You don't build a career terminating poor performers. You build a successful career by helping people be successful." Make no mistake, he did want performance, but he cared deeply about the people doing the work.

On a personal note, my youngest son, David, is disabled. Truett knew this and for two decades after David's birth, I don't remember a single encounter with him that he didn't ask me about David. All you needed to do was to spend a few minutes with Truett to know he cared about results *and* relationships.

Embody a Leader's Heart—Leadership character can be formed and strengthened at any stage in your life. For Truett, the process began early in his childhood.

When Truett was a child, his teacher asked each student to select a verse from the Bible to be submitted as the verse of the day. Because of Truett's speech impediment and to help him avoid the trauma of sharing his verse aloud, his mom wrote a verse on a slip of paper for him. The next day, Truett handed the piece of paper to his teacher. He was thrilled when his verse was selected as the verse of the week and written on the chalkboard for all to see.

A good name is more desirable than great riches.
Proverbs 22:1

From that moment until his last day, this would become his life's verse. Truett's leadership character was being formed at an early age.

IMPACT BEYOND OUR LIFETIME

You may not be the type of person who gives much thought to your legacy. Even if you've never considered the impact your life and leadership will have on those around you and the world at large, I want you to, even if just for a moment.

Legacy is what we leave behind that lasts. Yes, we'll leave our physical possessions behind. These things are not what I'm talking about. Most of them really don't matter and won't last that long—the cars will break down and houses will be sold. The thing that lasts is the impact we had on the people in this world, the people we knew and influenced and those who will be influenced by our work after we are gone. What will they say about you? How will they feel about your influence on their life? In his book *The Gift of Influence*, my friend Tommy Spaulding challenged me with the following big idea.

Most people meet three new people every day. If you live a normal life expectancy, that means you will meet eighty thousand new people in your life. Imagine just before your death, you can meet all these people. They have gathered in any one of twenty stadiums across America capable of holding a crowd of this size. As you walk to the 50-yard line to address the crowd, what will their reaction be? Will they cheer, jeer, or remain indifferent? The actions you and I take today, and every day, will determine their reaction. That's why my encouragement to you is to lead every day.

As I think about Truett's life, I'm sure he influenced tens of millions of people. To work with him was a real gift. I am part of his legacy, and if you embrace any of the ideas from this book, you are too!

Someone asked where I thought I would be if I had not worked at Chick-fil-A. I think the more thought-provoking question is, *Who* would I be? I was not only influenced by Truett but by hundreds of other leaders within our organization who understood and modeled Uncommon Leadership. They are all my heroes.

You and I will likely never amass the fame or fortune of a Truett Cathy, but Uncommon Greatness doesn't require either. It does require intentionality. It also requires us to rise above the misconceptions of the world around us. Uncommon Greatness is ultimately measured by the impact we have on those around us. For those of us striving to leave this world a better place, this should be great news—this form of greatness is still within our reach, and we can show others the way as well.

IMPACT TODAY AND TOMORROW

How do you begin, or continue to build, your legacy starting today? If you go back through the pages you've just read, I trust you'll have ample ideas regarding your next steps. My advice can be summarized with a simple recap of the Fundamentals of Uncommon Leadership. If you want to leave a legacy that lasts and take steps toward Uncommon Greatness, my encouragement to you is to SERVE.

See the Future
Engage and Develop Others
Reinvent Continuously
Value Results and Relationships
Embody a Leader's Heart

This is the leader's path to Uncommon Greatness regardless of your sphere of influence. You can SERVE at home, in your school, in your local community, at nonprofit organizations, and in your workplace.

For a leader to SERVE has always been countercultural and, honestly, uncommon. However, when consistently done well, this approach will produce superior results over time. As George Washington Carver said:

> *When you can do the common things of life in an uncommon way, you will command the attention of the world.*

When you apply these Fundamentals of Uncommon Leadership to your most pressing challenges and opportunities, you'll not only command the attention of the world; you'll also change yours!

Resources

I trust you found value in what you've just read. Some of you have already identified your next steps to become a better leader—congratulations! For others, you may need additional information or assistance.

One of the resources our team created to help you clarify your next steps is the Uncommon Greatness Digital Assessment. It's **FREE**. You have three options for accessing the assessment:

1. Text **uncommon** to 66866.
2. Go directly to the site: **uncommon.LeadEveryDay.com**.
3. Use this QR code:

Regardless of what's next for you, our team has created many other resources to serve you on your journey. We have additional books, field guides, assessments, videos, and more to help you become a better leader, strengthen your team, and build your own great organization. We also offer coaching, consulting, and training, all customized to meet your individual needs. You'll find a complete list of our resources and services at **LeadEveryDay.com**.

Acknowledgments

This is one of my favorite parts of writing a book! I have an opportunity to introduce you to the men and women who helped bring this work to life. On this project, the list of contributors has been written over a couple of decades! As I mentioned in the introduction, I had the privilege to assemble a team years ago to help Chick-fil-A figure out what we believed about leadership. This was the first step on a long march that continues today to create a leadership culture.

The following folks helped start that ball rolling for Chick-fil-A on this critical quest over twenty-five years ago: **Lee Burn**, **Mark Conklin**, **Cynthia Cornog**, **Lance Lanier**, and **Phil Orazi**. Thank you for your insights, diligence, wisdom, discernment, and spirit of collaboration. Together, we created something that will continue to serve leaders for decades to come. *Uncommon Greatness* is an extension of *your* growing legacy.

I also want to thank **Chick-fil-A's Executive Committee** from more than two decades ago for supporting Ken Blanchard's crazy idea for the two of us to write *The Secret*. Your response still inspires me today. They said, "We think you should write the book. Maybe it will serve the world." I've rarely seen a better example of an abundance mentality. None of us anticipated that book to be translated into twenty-five languages. Thanks for your vision and leadership.

I must also thank **Ken Blanchard**. I dedicated this book to you. I'll never forget the day I shared with you the work that our team had done to articulate our leadership point of view. The first words out of your mouth were, "This has got to be a book!" I know I dismissed that idea in the moment. Thanks for your intuition and persistence. Together, we have served leaders around the world with this content. Also, thanks for showing me what a true servant leader looks like.

To **Steve Piersanti** and the team at Berrett-Koehler, thanks for publishing *The Secret* and stewarding the process of more than two dozen translations. Thanks to your efforts, leaders around the world were exposed to a life-changing message in their own language. The fruit of your efforts will reverberate for generations.

Moving to the present day, we once again had the chance to build amazing research, editorial, and publishing teams. I wish we could quantify the impact your work is going to have on the world in the years to come. You have not only made this work possible; you made it fantastic! We wanted to hear from thousands of leaders around the world, and you rounded them up. We wanted fresh exemplars of the concepts in the book, and you found them. We wanted to do all of this on an impossible deadline, and yet, you rose to the challenge. Thank you!

Content and Research Team—Truth is always transformational, if you can articulate it in a fashion that is approachable and actionable. Just because *Uncommon Greatness* is built on timeless principles, this did not minimize the rigor this team demonstrated during our research phase. For those who missed it, the team interviewed or surveyed more than four thousand leaders from six countries. Then, of course, we had the opportunity to unpack all the data—it was like Christmas morning! Here are the people who designed the research, conducted interviews, and/or mined the data for the insights.

Nicole Williams led the overall project team. It was my first chance to work with Nicole. My only regret is that we haven't worked on dozens of projects together over the years. Your talent is evident to all who know you. Additional key contributors included **Claire Jervis**, **Mike Johnson**, **Erin Weissert**, **Uyen Dang**, **Jesse Shea**, **Freddy Fang**, **Jillian Broaddus**, **Mike Fleming**, and **Jessica Everett**. You guys are rock stars. Thank you!

Editorial Team—As usual with my books, a lot of people helped craft the rough ideas and crude manuscript into something that we can all be proud of. I'll start with **Mike Johnson**. This is the second time his name has shown up here because he wore multiple hats over the course of this project. Regarding editorial, I've said this before—MJ is a better writer than I am. Your patience with me during the process was greatly appreciated. I look forward to helping you write your first book in the near future.

Janice Rutledge, you are amazing! This is the eleventh book you've helped me write. Thanks for your willingness to keep coming back for more. As I've told you privately, I don't ever intend to write another book without your assistance. Your insights and instincts are phenomenal. Your skills are demonstrated on virtually every page of *Uncommon Greatness*. The readability of the final product is a testimony to your talent. Thank you!

Katie Dickman, you were the wizard behind the curtain for this manuscript. You knew exactly where to push, probe, and question the early drafts. Of all your powers, clarity is your greatest gift to me. Rather than providing it, you most often forced me to search for it. Sorry you had to do that so often. Our readers will be forever grateful you prevented them from having to read my mind throughout this book!

Reviewers—I've already referenced the timeline for this book. To pull it off, we enlisted multiple reviewers. I want to thank each one of you. Here's the list of folks who reviewed all or part of the manuscript:

Ron Acosta, Jillian Broaddus, Beth Dahlenburg, Brittany Daniels, Randy Gravitt, Morris Jackson, Eddie Kober, Norm Kober, Martha Lawrence, Andy Lorenzen, Lauren McGuire, Casey Meadows, Donna Miller, Justin Miller, David Oakes, Tracy Polite-Johnson, Jonathan Purser, Cliff Robinson, Tim Tassopoulos, Rob Taylor, Zach Thomas, K.J. and Anna Wari, and **Kevin Williams.**

Publishing & Design Team—Thanks to **Matt Holt** and BenBella Books for believing in a guy who sold chicken for a living. Your partnership has allowed leaders around the world to be strengthened. Thanks to **Katie Dickman, Michael Fedison, Brigid Pearson**, and **Lindsay Miller**. Thanks to **Alex Field** from the Bindery Agency for the introduction to Matt and team!

Digital Assessment Team—I hope everyone reading this will check out the digital assessment (in case you missed the references throughout the book, here's the link one more time: uncommon.LeadEveryDay.com). This team worked miracles to get this done on a very aggressive timeline. Based on the positive feedback I've already received, I'm counting on this being a game changer for leaders everywhere. Thanks to **Nicole Williams, Erin Weissert, Jenna Wang, Uyen Dang, Adrienne Barnett, Ben McCraw, Kyle Schultz, Asha Kucht, Andrew Bonnenfant, Guillermo Riojas, Freddy Espana, Antonio Ixtecoc, A.J. Slizeski, Mike Johnson, Ben McCraw, Jessica Everett,** and **Ben Kubany** for making this life-changing tool available to the world.

Additional Resources Team—One of the challenges our team takes very seriously is how to help leaders apply the content in a book like this. Hopefully, the Ideas for Action chapters will give you a head start. However, for some of you, you'll want more. If you do, the Uncommon Greatness Field Guide and Quick Start Guide may be helpful. As you can imagine, the creation of these resources was also a team effort. Thanks to **Randy Gravitt, Jillian Broaddus, Lindsay Miller,** and **Bonita Darden** for making these resources a reality. In addition to being extremely pragmatic, they are well written and beautifully designed and printed—a powerful combination! If you're interested, you can find them at LeadEveryDay.com.

Marketing & Social Media Team—I want to proactively thank **Becky Robinson, Wendy Haan, Mallory Hyde, Zach Clark, Micah Foster, Elizabeth Mars, Amy Driehorst,** and **Jaimee Roy.** They will get the word out to the world about this book. On my last book, *Culture Rules,* they landed us on the *Wall Street Journal* Bestseller List. I know you'll do a great job sharing *Uncommon Greatness* with the world.

Research Participants—If you are one of the thousands of leaders we surveyed or interviewed, thank you! We worked diligently to ensure your voice, issues, and thoughts were woven into the fabric of this project. Although your name doesn't appear here, you are a very real part of this work. It's my desire that you'll benefit from the work you helped create.

Air Traffic Control—Special thanks to **Brittany Miller**, who helped steward my time and manage the thousands of details associated with this work—the meetings, interviews, travel, and more. Your contributions were huge!

Notes

INTRODUCTION

1. Lana and Lilly Wachowski, *The Matrix,* Warner Bros., 1999.

CHOOSE A DIFFERENT PATH

1. "What Drives Global Engagement," Marcus Buckingham website, May 13, 2019, https://www.marcusbuckingham.com/what-drives -global-engagement/.
2. "Growth & Innovation," McKinsey website, accessed May 26, 2023, https://www.mckinsey.com/capabilities/strategy-and-corporate -finance/how-we-help-clients/growth-and-innovation.
3. Randall J. Beck and Jim Harter, "Why Great Managers Are Rare," Gallup website, accessed May 26, 2023, https://www.gallup.com /workplace/231593/why-great-managers-rare.aspx.
4. "Gartner Says 45% of Managers Lack Confidence to Help Employees Develop the Skills They Need Today," Gartner press release, September 18, 2019, https://www.gartner.com/en/newsroom/press-releases/2019 -09-18-gartner-says-45--of-managers-lack-confidence-to-help-.
5. Ryan Pendell, "The World's $7.8 Trillion Workplace Problem," Gallup website, June 14, 2022, https://www.gallup.com/workplace/393497 /world-trillion-workplace-problem.aspx.

6. Prophet / Chick-fil-A Leadership Quantitative Study, May 2023.

7. Ibid.

8. Jim Collins, Jerry Porras, *Built to Last* (New York: Harper Business Essentials, 2002).

SEE THE UNSEEN

1. "Wendy Kopp," Academy of Achievement website, accessed April 26, 2022, https://achievement.org/achiever/wendy-kopp/.

2. Wendy Kopp, *One Day, All Children: The Unlikely Triumph of Teach For America and What I Learned Along the Way* (New York: PublicAffairs, 2001).

3. "Wendy Kopp," Academy of Achievement website.

4. Ibid.

5. "Wendy Kopp Interview," Academy of Achievement website, accessed April 26, 2022, https://achievement.org/achiever/wendy-kopp/#interview.

6. "What We Do—The Challenge," Teach For America website, accessed April 26, 2022, https://www.teachforamerica.org/what-we-do/challenge.

7. Stacey Childress, "Teach For America 2005," *Harvard Business Review*, March 2, 2005.

8. Elisa Villanueva Beard, "Inspired by the Next Generation," Teach For America website, May 1, 2017, https://www.teachforamerica.org/top-stories/elisa-villanueva-beard-inspired-by-the-next-generation.

9. Alexandra Hootnick, "Teachers Are Losing Their Jobs, but Teach For America's Expanding. What's Wrong with That?," The Nation website, April 15, 2015, https://www.thenation.com/article/archive/teachers-are-losing-their-jobs-teach-americas-expanding-whats-wrong/#:~:text=In%202011%2C%20TFA%20founder%20Wendy,tear%20the%20whole%20thing%20apart.%E2%80%9D.

10. "What We Do—The Challenge," Teach For America website, accessed April 26, 2022, https://www.teachforamerica.org/what-we-do/challenge.

11. "Teach For All," Teach For All homepage, accessed April 26, 2022, https://teachforall.org/.

12. Rachel Makinson, "Jeff Bezos: The Inspirational Success Story of Amazon's Founder," https://www.ceotodaymagazine.com/2022/07/jeff-bezos-the-inspirational-success-story-of-amazons-founder/.

13. Ibid.

14. Laurel Wamsley, "Liftoff! Jeff Bezos and 3 Crewmates Travel to Space and Back in Under 15 Minutes," NPR website, July 20, 2021, https://www.npr.org/2021/07/20/1018279093/jeff-bezos-blue-origin-space-flight.

15. Fields Wicker-Miurin, "Learning from Leadership's Missing Manual," TED website, 2009, https://www.ted.com/talks/fields_wicker_miurin_learning_from_leadership_s_missing_manual?language=en.

16. Ibid.

17. "Benki Piyãko Ashaninka," Aquaverde website, accessed May 1, 2023, https://www.aquaverde.org/en/benki-piyako-ashaninka/.

SEE THE FUTURE: IDEAS FOR ACTION

1. Thomas G. West, *Plato's 'Apology of Socrates,' an Interpretation, with a New Translation* (Ithaca, NY: Cornell University Press, 1979).

2. "Transcript: Making the Most of Your After Action Review," Justice Clearinghouse website, accessed April 27, 2022, https://www.justiceclearinghouse.com/transcript-making-the-most-of-your-after-action-review/.

3. Marcus Tullius Cicero, "De Divinatione (On Divination)," Book II, Chapter LII, Section 90, 44 BC.

4. Mark Perry, "Only 52 US Companies Have Been on the Fortune 500 Since 1955, Thanks to the 'Creative Destruction' That Fuels Economic Prosperity," American Enterprise Institute website, June 3, 2021, https://www.aei.org/carpe-diem/only-52-us-companies-have-been-on-the-fortune-500-since-1955-thanks-to-the-creative-destruction-that-fuels-economic-prosperity-2/.

5. Edward de Bono, *Six Thinking Hats* (Boston: Back Bay Books, 1999).

6. "Savannah Bananas: The 5 E's to Creating Raving Fans," YouTube, Jesse Cole—The Yellow Tux Guy, January 27, 2022, https://www.youtube.com/watch?v=_OMEfsq6HRA.

BECOME UNSTOPPABLE

1. Eric Schmidt, Jonathan Rosenberg, and Alan Eagle, *Trillion Dollar Coach* (New York: HarperCollins, 2019).

2. Ibid.

3. Ibid.

4. Ibid.

5. Ibid.

6. Ibid.

7. Ibid.

8. Ibid.

9. Noah Davis and Michael Lopez, "Don't Be Fooled by Baseball's Small-Budget Success Stories," FiveThirtyEight, July 8, 2015, https://fivethirtyeight.com/features/dont-be-fooled-by-baseballs-small-budget-success-stories/.

10. Grant Shorin, *Team Payroll Versus Performance in Professional Sports: Is Increased Spending Associated with Greater Success?,* honors thesis, Duke University, 2017, https://hdl.handle.net/10161/14332.

11. Wyan Wan and Joshua Gunawan, *Does Money Mean Success in the English Premier League?,* Bruin Sports Analytics website, June 15, 2021, https://www.bruinsportsanalytics.com/post/money_in_epl.

12. Jim Harter, "Globally, Employees Are More Engaged—and More Stressed," Gallup, June 13, 2023, https://www.gallup.com/workplace/506798/globally-employees-engaged-stressed.aspx.

13. Brian J. Brim and Jim Asplund, "The Powerful Duo of Strengths and Engagement," Gallup, May 9, 2023, https://www.gallup.com/workplace/505523/powerful-duo-strengths-engagement.aspx.

14. Aaron Skonnard, "The Most Important Culture Change You Can Make," *Inc.* magazine website, December 16, 2014, https://www.inc.com/aaron-skonnard/the-most-important-culture-change-you-can-make.html.

15. Personal interview with Jack Stack, CEO, Springfield Remanufacturing Corp. (SRC).

16. Ibid.

17. Ibid.

18. Jack Stack and Bo Burlingham, *The Great Game of Business* (Sydney: Currency, 2013).

19. Jaime Escalante and Jack Dirmann, "The Jaime Escalante Math Program," *Journal of Negro Education* 59, no. 3 (1990), 407–23.

20. Ibid.

21. Ibid.

22. "Jaime Alfonso Escalante," School of Mathematics and Statistics at University of St. Andrews, Scotland archives, accessed April 27, 2023, https://mathshistory.st-andrews.ac.uk/Biographies/Escalante/.

23. Ibid.

24. Ibid.

25. Escalante and Dirmann, "The Jaime Escalante Math Program," 407–23.

ENGAGE AND DEVELOP OTHERS: IDEAS FOR ACTION

1. "Guide: Understand Team Effectiveness," Google re:Work website, accessed May 1, 2023, https://rework.withgoogle.com/print/guides/5721312655835136/.

2. Charles "Chic" Thompson, *What a Great Idea* (New York: Harper Perennial, 1992).

3. Costantino Nivola, born Orani, Italy, 1911, died Southampton, NY, 1988, Digital Public Library of America, http://collections.si.edu/search/results.htm?q=record_ID=saam_1984.124.227&repo=DPLA.

4. Jon Katzenbach and Douglas Smith, *The Wisdom of Teams* (Cambridge, MA: Harvard Business Press Review, 2015).

5. John Kostoulas, "Technologies Are Critical for Inclusion in the Workplace," Gartner blog post, August 30, 2018, https://blogs.gartner.com/john-kostoulas/2018/08/30/technologies-critical-for-inclusion/#:~:text=Gartner%20research%20reveals%20that%20inclusive,structured%20interventions%20across%20the%20organization.

6. Glassdoor Team, "Diversity & Inclusion Workplace Survey," Glassdoor blog post, September 30, 2020, https://www.glassdoor.com/employers /blog/diversity-inclusion-workplace-survey/.

7. Frans Johansson, *The Medici Effect* (Cambridge, MA: Harvard Business School Press, 2006).

8. "How Microsoft 'Screens-In' Culture Change: Kathleen Hogan," Gartner podcast, September 13, 2016, https://www.gartner.com/en /podcasts/talent-angle/how-microsoft-screens-in-culture-change.

9. Peter Drucker, *The Five Most Important Questions You Will Ever Ask About Your Organization* (Hoboken, NJ: Jossey-Bass, 2008).

10. John Kotter, "Leading Change: Why Transformation Efforts Fail," *Harvard Business Review* website, accessed April 27, 2023, https://hbr .org/1995/05/leading-change-why-transformation-efforts-fail-2.

11. Howard Gardner, *Multiple Intelligences: New Horizons* (New York: Basic Books, 2006).

ESCAPE THE NORM

1. "MrBeast," Social Blade website, accessed April 30, 2023, https:// socialblade.com/youtube/user/mrbeast6000.

2. Jimmy Donaldson, "$456,000 Squid Game in Real Life!," YouTube, uploaded by MrBeast, November 24, 2021, https://www.youtube.com /watch?v=0e3GPea1Tyg.

3. Jimmy Donaldson, "Going Through the Same Drive Thru 1,000 Times!," YouTube, uploaded by MrBeast, October 5, 2019, https:// www.youtube.com/watch?v=QxGVgXf_LNk.

4. Esha Singh, "When Did MrBeast Start His YouTube Channel? Growth Explored as YouTuber Hits 100 Million Subscribers," SK Pop blog post, July 29, 2022, https://www.sportskeeda.com/pop-culture /when-mrbeast-start-youtube-channel-growth-explored-youtuber-hits -100-million-subscribers.

5. Jimmy Donaldson, "1,000 Blind People See for the First Time," YouTube, uploaded by MrBeast, January 28, 2023, https://www .youtube.com/watch?v=TJ2ifmkGGus&t=339s.

6. Stephen Findeisen, "Mr. Beast's Secret Formula for Going Viral," YouTube, uploaded by Coffeezilla, December 21, 2021, https://www.youtube.com/watch?v=6pMhBaG81MI.

7. Lex Fridman, "MrBeast's advice for new YouTube creators," YouTube, uploaded by Lex Clips, January 13, 2023, https://www.youtube.com/watch?v=rbmYbAPGBu8.

8. Lex Fridman, "MrBeast: How to Hire a Great Team," YouTube, uploaded by Lex Clips, January 14, 2023, https://www.youtube.com/watch?v=ROhcX7Y5JhI&t=213s.

9. Logan Paul, "How Mr. Beast Brainstorms Crazy Ideas," YouTube, uploaded by IMPAULSIVE Clips, November 19, 2019, https://www.youtube.com/watch?v=zBTvx0_Q1g4.

10. "MrBeast Teaches at Harvard Business School," MrBeast News website, April 13, 2023, https://mrbeastburger.io/mrbeast-teaches-at-harvard-business-school/.

11. Michele Theil, "MrBeast Said He Turned Down $1 Billion Deal for His YouTube Channel and Associated Companies," *Business Insider* website, September 28, 2022, https://www.insider.com/mr-beast-turned-down-1-billion-dollar-deal-youtuber-2022-9.

12. "MrBeast Teaches at Harvard Business School."

13. Joe Guszkowski, "MrBeast Burger Is Opening a Brick-and-Mortar Restaurant," *Restaurant Business* website, August 30, 2022, https://www.restaurantbusinessonline.com/emerging-brands/mrbeast-burger-opening-brick-mortar-restaurant.

14. Arianna Huffington, *Thrive* (New York: Harmony, 2015).

15. Arianna Huffington, *The Sleep Revolution* (New York: Harmony, 2016).

16. "Manchester United Football Club Built a 200-Million-Euro Facility with 80 Sleeping Rooms for the Team to Use Before Every Home Game," BBC website, December 8, 2014, https://www.bbc.com/sport/football/30376774.

17. Mike Tanier, "Next Big Thing: Sleep Science Is Becoming the NFL's Secret Weapon," Bleacher Report website, October 5, 2016, https://bleacherreport.com/articles/2650188-next-big-thing-sleep-science-is-becoming-the-nfls-secret-weapon.

18. "Casper-Gallup State of Sleep in America 2022 Report," Gallup website, accessed April 30, 2023, https://www.gallup.com/analytics/390536/sleep-in-america-2022.aspx.

19. "Great British Sleep Survey 2012," Sleepio website, accessed April 30, 2023, https://www.sleepio.com/2012report/.

20. K. D. Kochanek, S. L. Murphy, J. Xu, and E. Arias, *Mortality in the United States,* 2013, NCHS Data Briefs 178 (2014):1–8.

21. Eddie Allen, "Sir Dave Brailsford at British Cycling—A Career Retrospective," British Cycling website, April 11, 2014, https://www.britishcycling.org.uk/gbcyclingteam/article/gbr20140411-British-Cycling---The-Brailsford-years-0.

22. Eben Harrell, "How 1% Performance Improvements Led to Olympic Gold," *Harvard Business Review* website, October 30, 2015, https://hbr.org/2015/10/how-1-performance-improvements-led-to-olympic-gold.

23. Alan Wess, "Compound Interest," Alan Weiss website, March 14, 2018, https://alanweiss.com/compound-interest/.

24. James Clear, *Atomic Habits* (New York: Avery, 2018).

25. Peter Fisk, "Marginal Gains," Peter Fisk website, March 20, 2019, https://www.peterfisk.com/2019/03/marginal-gains-alcohol-on-bike-tyres-and-electrically-heated-shorts-from-cycling-to-marathon-running-education-and-healthcare-1-improvement-can-make-a-big-difference/.

26. Eben Harrell, "How 1% Performance Improvements Led to Olympic Gold," *Harvard Business Review* website, October 30, 2015, https://hbr.org/2015/10/how-1-performance-improvements-led-to-olympic-gold.

27. Eddie Allen, "Sir Dave Brailsford at British Cycling—A Career Retrospective."

REINVENT CONTINUOUSLY: IDEAS FOR ACTION

1. Apple, "Here's to the Crazy Ones," YouTube, uploaded by VintageMacMuseum, May 23, 2010, https://www.youtube.com/watch?v=tjgtLSHhTPg.

2. Charles "Chic" Thompson, *What a Great Idea* (New York: Harper Perennial, 1992).

3. Dr. Edward de Bono, personal website, https://www.debono.com/.

RELEASE THE POWER

1. "Our History," WD-40 website, accessed April 27, 2023, https://www.wd40company.com/our-company/our-history/.

2. Ibid.

3. Garry Ridge, "The WD-40 Company Tribe Story: How We Turned a Great Company into a Community of Belonging," LinkedIn post, July 7, 2018, https://www.linkedin.com/pulse/wd-40-company-tribe-story-how-we-turned-great-community-garry-ridge/.

4. Ken Blanchard and Garry Ridge, *Helping People Win at Work* (New York: Pearson, 2009).

5. Ibid.

6. Ibid.

7. "Fascinating Facts You Never Learned in School," WD-40 website, accessed April 27, 2023, https://www.wd40.com/history/.

8. Garry Ridge, "The WD-40 Company Tribe Story: How We Turned a Great Company into a Community of Belonging," LinkedIn post, July 7, 2018, https://www.linkedin.com/pulse/wd-40-company-tribe-story-how-we-turned-great-community-garry-ridge/.

9. Jim Collins and Jerry Porras, *Built to Last* (New York: Harper Business, 2002).

10. Adam Parr and Ross Brawn, *Total Competition* (London: Simon & Schuster, 2016).

11. Ibid.

12. Ibid.

13. Personal interview with former Ferrari engineer, April 29, 2021.

14. Parr and Brawn, *Total Competition*.

15. "William T. 'Bill' Walton," Basketball Hall of Fame biographies, accessed April 27, 2023, https://www.hoophall.com/hall-of-famers/bill-walton/.

16. Bill Walton, *Back from the Dead* (New York: Simon & Schuster, 2017).

17. "The Pyramid of SUCCESS," The Wooden Effect website, accessed April 27, 2023, https://www.thewoodeneffect.com/pyramid-of-success/.

VALUE RESULTS AND RELATIONSHIPS: IDEAS FOR ACTION

1. Personal interview with Jason Williamson, February 24, 2021.
2. Paul Hersey, Ken Blanchard, and Dewey Johnson, *Management of Organizational Behavior: Leading Human Resources,* 9th ed. (Upper Saddle River, NJ: Pearson Prentice Hall, 2008).
3. "Bersin & Associates Unlocks the Secrets of Effective Employee Recognition," PRNewsWire website, June 12, 2012, https://www.prnewswire.com/news-releases/bersin--associates-unlocks-the-secrets-of-effective-employee-recognition-158548395.html.
4. "One Third of Your Life Is Spent at Work," Gettysburg College website, accessed May 1, 2023, https://www.gettysburg.edu/news/stories?id=79db7b34-630c-4f49-ad32-4ab9ea48e72b&pageTitle=1%2F3+of+your+life+is+spent+at+work.

LEAD WITH HEART

1. Catherine Clinton, "'General Tubman': Female Abolitionist Was Also a Secret Military Weapon," *Military Times* archives, February 7, 2018, https://www.militarytimes.com/military-honor/black-military-history/2018/02/07/general-tubman-female-abolitionist-was-also-a-secret-military-weapon/.
2. Paul Donnelly, "Harriet Tubman's Great Raid," *New York Times* archives, June 7, 2013, https://archive.nytimes.com/opinionator.blogs.nytimes.com/2013/06/07/harriet-tubmans-great-raid/.
3. "Harriet Tubman," History.com, last modified March 29, 2023, https://www.history.com/topics/black-history/harriet-tubman.
4. Clinton, "'General Tubman.'"
5. Ibid.
6. Debra Michals, "Harriet Tubman," National Women's History Museum website, accessed April 28, 2023, https://www.womenshistory.org/education-resources/biographies/harriet-tubman.
7. Janell Hobson, "The Breathtaking Courage of Harriet Tubman—Janell

Hobson," YouTube, uploaded by TED-Ed, July 24, 2018, https://www
.youtube.com/watch?v=Dv7YhVKFqbQ.

8. "Peter Drucker Quotes About Character," AZ Quotes website, accessed
April 30, 2023, https://www.azquotes.com/author/4147-Peter_Drucker
/tag/character.

9. Frances Hesselbein, *My Life in Leadership* (Hoboken, NJ: Jossey-Bass,
2011).

10. Frances Hesselbein and General Eric Shinseki, *Be, Know, Do* (Boston:
Jossey-Bass, 2004).

11. Hesselbein, *My Life in Leadership*.

12. "Frances Hesselbein, a Pitt Visionary and One of the World's 'Greatest
Leaders,' Has Died at 107," University of Pittsburgh PittWire website,
December 11, 2022, https://www.pitt.edu/pittwire/features-articles
/frances-hesselbein-obituary.

EMBODY A LEADER'S HEART: IDEAS FOR ACTION

1. Matt Kelly, "Historians: The Full Story of D-Day Is More Complex Than the Myth," University of Virginia UVAToday website,
June 5, 2019, https://news.virginia.edu/content/historians-full-story
-d-day-more-complex-myth.

2. Srinivas Rao, "Unmistakable Classics: Seth Godin | The Emotional Jour-
ney of Shipping Creative Work," *The Unmistakable Creative Podcast,* November 25, 2020, https://podcasts.apple.com/us/podcast/unmistakable
-classics-seth-godin-the-emotional/id352721366?i=1000534443678.

3. Martin E. P. Seligman, *Learned Optimism* (New York: A.A. Knopf,
1991).

4. "Jack Nicklaus—Golf Quotes from The Golden Bear," Your Golf
Travel website, accessed June 16, 2023, https://www.yourgolftravel
.com/19th-hole/jack-nicklaus-golf-quotes-from-the-golden-bear/.

5. Olivier Poirier-Leroy, "How Michael Phelps Used Visualization to Stay
Calm Under Pressure," Your Swim Log website, accessed June 16, 2023,
https://www.yourswimlog.com/michael-phelps-visualization/.

6. James Kerr, "How Bill Belichick's 'Do Your Job' Mantra Applies to

Leadership," *Inc.* magazine website, January 26, 2015, https://www.inc .com/james-kerr/how-do-your-job-can-be-a-difference-maker-for-your -company.html.

7. Brené Brown, "The Power of Vulnerability," TED, January 3, 2011, https://www.ted.com/talks/brene_brown_the_power_of_vulnerability/c.

8. David Goggins, *Never Finished* (Carson City, NV: Lioncrest Publishing, 2021).

9. John Maxwell, *Failing Forward* (Nashville: Thomas Nelson, 2022).

10. Malcolm Gladwell, *The Tipping Point* (New York: Back Bay Books, 2002).

11. Jacob Morgan, *The Future Leader* (Hoboken, NJ: Wiley, 2020).

Index

About the Author

Mark Miller is a seasoned business leader, a *Wall Street Journal* and international best-selling author, and a dynamic communicator. He worked for one of the world's great organizations for almost forty-five years. Mark began his Chick-fil-A career as an hourly team member and recently retired as the Vice President, High Performance Leadership.

Mark began his Chick-fil-A career working in one of the chain's local restaurants as an hourly employee. He then joined the corporate staff working in the warehouse and mailroom. Since those early days, Mark has provided leadership for Corporate Communications, Field Operations, Training & Development, Quality and Customer Satisfaction, Leadership Development, and more. For the last twenty-five years, much of his time has been focused on helping the organization grow its leadership capacity.

Mark and his team at Chick-fil-A have invested a quarter century and millions of dollars searching for and validating ideas that work. Over the years, they have focused on numerous topics including building High Performance Teams, High Performance Organizations, Employee Engagement, Execution, Personal Leadership Effectiveness, and most recently, Culture. These projects have each culminated in globally acclaimed books. Today, more than one million copies of Mark's books are available in twenty-five translations around the world . . . and counting!

Mark's passion is serving leaders. His content is simple without being simplistic, pragmatic, and life changing. He has traveled to dozens of countries around the globe to encourage and equip leaders to change their world.

Mark is also an avid photographer. His expeditions have taken him to some of the world's most difficult-to-reach destinations. He has photographed silverback gorillas in the jungles of Rwanda, icebergs in Antarctica, Maasai warriors in East Africa, Nepalese culture at Everest Base Camp, and much more. New adventures are in the works.

Mark is married to Donna, his high school sweetheart. They recently celebrated their fortieth wedding anniversary. Mark and Donna have two sons, Justin and David. Justin is married to Lindsay; their children, Addie, Logan, and Finn, are frequently featured on Mark's Instagram feed.

Mark would love to connect with you and talk about how he can serve you or your team! Visit his website, **LeadEveryDay .com**, for rich content, free resources, links to his social channels, and more. You can also call or text Mark at **678-612-8441**.